LIFE AFTER

50

A POSITIVE LOOK AT AGING IN THE FAITH COMMUNITY

Edited by Katie Funk Wiebe

Preface by Erland Waltner

Faith and Life Press, Newton, Kansas

*L*ife *After 50* seeks to educate and inspire middle-aged and older adults in the faith community to see aging as a process that is both challenge and grace. This book is not a "how-to-grow-old-gracefully" book, but a challenge to achieve meaning, maintain hope, and continue to serve, through being and doing as long as possible, and solely through being as the years advance.

Printed in the United States of America

96 95 94 93 4 3 2 1

Library of Congress Number 92-74439

International Standard Book Number 0-87303-203-9

Editorial direction for Faith and Life Press by Susan E. Janzen; copyediting by Edna Krueger Dyck; design by John Hiebert; printing by Mennonite Press.

TABLE OF CONTENTS

PREFACE

Whether we see our life pilgrimage as a journey into the light or as a journey into the darkness makes all the difference in the world. While the Bible recognizes both the delights and challenges of the life journey, the inspired Old Testament sage observes that "the path of the righteous is like the first gleam of dawn, shining ever brighter till the full light of day" (Prov. 4:18, NIV). He implies that, in some matters, we may choose what we become.

To inquire into the meaning of *aging* is to inquire into the nature and meaning of human life. This inquiry is not only appropriate but imperative at every stage of the life cycle and needs to be confronted in terms appropriate to each stage. In this process, the *faith community*, meaning the church, potentially contributes a decisive difference.

This publication arises out of concerns of the Inter-Mennonite Council on Aging, later known as the Mennonite Association of Retired Persons (MARP), and the Mennonite Health Association (MHA) calling for new dialogue on aging in the faith community. Two conferences on this theme convened in June 1992, one at Messiah College, Grantham, Pennsylvania, and one at Goshen College, Goshen, Indiana.

Those persons asking for new dialogue recognized that aging, as a way of describing the life journey, has its physical, psychological, social, economic, and even ecological dimensions. However, they viewed growing older particularly as a spiritual journey, that is, a conscious relationship of human beings with God, in which faith, love, and hope are strategic ingredients.

The purpose of the inter-Mennonite conferences on aging became the background for this publication, namely:

* To assist congregations to enlarge their vision of the aging process in view of the increased longevity of American people.

* To empower congregations to develop an awareness of spiritual resources for meaningful living for older persons in the face of economic and technological issues.

* To inform and equip congregations and older persons to address ethical choices in their midst in the context of the faith community and our spiritual heritage.

This publication was early envisioned as a means of sharing with congregations and with the larger faith community the basic values and perspectives that emerged from the dialogue. This book not only explores the importance for faith people at every age to be concerned about their spiritual journey, but also suggests and provides resources to younger and older persons to increase and enhance the possibilities and delights of the aging journey. Katie Funk Wiebe of Wichita, Kansas, already widely appreciated for several published works on related themes, was chosen editor and core writer. An editorial board was set up to provide guidance and counsel.

Paul N. Kraybill, executive director of the Mennonite Health Association, was dominant in initiating and doing the early planning of the conferences on aging and of this publication. He has since suffered an incapacitating illness and has had to withdraw. This publication is affectionately and gratefully dedicated to him.

May God, as the Lord of the whole of human life, be pleased to bless this ministry inviting study, discussion, enrichment, and spiritual commitment for all among us who are "aging in the faith community."

Erland Waltner, Chair
Editorial Advisory Committee
Elkhart, Indiana
September 1992

INTRODUCTION

66 The faith community has a special responsibility or even obligation to perform with older adults," Elbert C. Cole, founder of the Shepherd's Centers of America, told the Fourteenth International Congress of Gerontology at Acapulco, Mexico, in 1989. This responsibility is to assure older adults not only of survival, but more importantly, to serve as their guide "on the journey of life, helping people find their meaning and purpose." Old age as an aspect of society that needs special attention is a recent phenomenon. Old people have been around since Adam and Eve, but until the middle of the twentieth century, when older adults were a small percentage of the total population, they were often integrated into the rest of society or remained part of an unexamined fringe.

Today older adults represent a large percentage of the population. Demographers estimate two-thirds of all persons who ever attained the age of sixty-five in the United States are still alive today. Older people today are healthier, more active, and more influential than any other older generation in history. As the boomer generation approaches fifty, their increasing numbers and longevity will produce a historic shift in the concerns, structure, and style of America, write Ken Dychtwald and Joe Flower in *Age Wave*.

As the editorial committee began its work, we recognized that the big question facing the church is to identify its role in this significant change sweeping society. Where are the spiritual resources to guide the church through this massive demographic change? Many agencies and institutions are concerned with maintenance-type issues—finances, housing, and health. What is the responsibility of the church to this growing group of older adults? and that of older adults to church and society? The church of Jesus Christ must take the next step, go beyond speaking to nuts-and-bolts issues and speak to spiritual concerns. With Cole I assert that older adults "can be directed in their search for meaning by the belief systems of the faith community."

Our goal, therefore, is to educate and inspire middle-aged and older adults in the faith community to see aging as a process that is both challenge and grace. The good news of the gospel should mean hope and grace for older adults, regardless of their circumstances. This book is not a "how-to-grow-old-gracefully" type of book, but a challenge to achieve meaning, maintain hope, and continue to serve, through being and doing as long as possible, and solely through being as the years advance.

The book begins with some basic information about growing older. The Bible, though not often seen as the guide to growing older, offers principles to direct our thinking. Sociologists and that growing group, the gerontologists, supply demographic facts and information about the social and political realities of our time that cannot be denied.

The book also tries to enhance the image the elderly have of themselves and their peer group. Older adults have been stereotyped as sick, poor, senile, and unproductive. Today a new stereotype is developing, one that views them as rich, indifferent to society's needs, and hedonistic. Neither image is correct. To change incorrect images requires seeing the members of this age group as unique individuals whose only common thread is their age.

Yet aging admittedly has its negative aspects; these should not be disregarded. But to focus on these makes aging a problem. The physical limitations faced by the older person are not the whole story, especially at a time when older people are living longer and with better health. The matter of meaning and purpose should be the overarching concern. In the local congregation that means accepting the challenge to discover anew and together, young and old, what God's purpose is for older adults in our communities. In Cole's words, faith must become intentional with this older group. Older adults are the prime evidence that the gospel works. If the gospel fails with them, it is not the gospel of truth.

This book provides the vehicle by which the topic of growing older can be comfortably and adequately introduced into the thinking of those approaching retirement years (the "fifty-plus" group) as well as those who have already moved into the post-"eight-to-five" workday years. We encouraged writers to keep the approach informal rather than academic.

As an editorial committee, we see the typical reader as a member of a faith community who is interested in planning for a meaningful life and service as an older adult or who is relating to older persons, whether these are parents, relatives, or friends. The book is addressed to "us," not to "them." We are all growing older and have been from the day we were born.

I recognize that the material in these chapters only begins to cover the vast subject of aging. The subject has many facets, and readers may wonder why certain topics were not included. The editorial committee recommended staying away from the highly technical questions related to housing, finances, legal issues, and so forth. These can be found in dozens of books on the subject. *The Growing Silver Resource: Functional Approach for Congregational Involvement with the Elderly* published by the Western District Conference (General Conference Mennonite Church) offers excellent practical suggestions for beginning a ministry to the older person.

This book moves in a different direction. It attempts to give the reader glimpses of new spiritual frontiers. We hope the reader will see aging not as an enemy to be conquered, but as a friend to be cultivated.

Certain topics come up in several chapters, which shows that life is a whole and can't be segmented by academic discipline. Several writers speak about the loss of identity after retirement and about death. The older woman, especially the woman who is single for any reason, is mentioned several times. Another voice you will hear often is the fervent call to the local congregation to be the church and to find its role with regard to the growing group of older adults. They can no longer be ignored.

We offer this material for personal enjoyment, for elective study in Sunday school classes and small study groups, as resource material for adult Christian education classes, college classes, and yes, even youth groups.

Acknowledgments: A special word of appreciation goes to Paul N. Kraybill, who spearheaded this project in its early stages until he became ill, and to his wife, Jean, who provided interim support to keep the project moving. The members of the editorial committee offered valuable advice in the planning stages: Erland Waltner, Ann Raber, Rick Stiffney, Stuart Showalter, Royce and Doris Engle, Herta Janzen, and Susan Janzen of Faith and Life Press. A note of appreciation goes to Lawrence H. Greaser, who stepped in with spirit and joy as interim coordinator for Mennonite Health Association. This book is the work of many persons. My thanks goes to each one.

Katie Funk Wiebe
Wichita, Kansas
September 1992

Dedicated to Paul N. Kraybill
who had a vision for this book

Part I

THE FOUNDATION

Many decades ago in high school geometry, we students learned theorems, or principles established as mathematical laws. We based our work on those principles and didn't dare stray from them at the risk of ending up in a grand confusion of figures and terms. We carefully cited these theorems as we moved through a problem. These were the foundation, or groundwork, of our calculations.

What are the foundations on which to base this study of life after middle age? While the Bible is not often considered as a source of theological understanding about aging, it is populated with many older people: Abraham and Sarah, Moses, and Simeon and Anna, to name a few. They teach us much about God's plan for older persons and how God related to them.

The demographics of our society cannot be dismissed as we think about the older adult. We are influenced by the trends in society through our conscious or subconscious awareness of them. A better knowledge of the influence of society upon us, including the mass media, can help us get rid of stereotyped thinking about aging.

These first four chapters lay the groundwork for the rest of the book, challenging you to think through what you know about aging and how you view it.

"The time has come," the Walrus says in Alice's Adventures in Wonderland, *"to talk of many things: of shoes–and ships–and sealing-wax–of cabbages–and kings." Within the faith community the time has come to speak about growing older. Whenever a new need arises in the church, the church has rallied to alleviate that need. Deacons were chosen in the early church to meet the needs of neglected widows. Women's work began to give women a ministry and to support missionary work. Sunday schools were first organized to train neglected street children. As young people, singles, and the handicapped became discernible groups within the church, it moved to meet their needs. The demographics of the church have changed again. This time the "new kid" on the block is the older adult, growing in number and vitality. How will the church respond?*

CHAPTER 1

IF YOU'RE GOING TO BE OLD, NOW IS THE TIME

Katie Funk Wiebe

Something important is happening among people in their later years—a ground swell, rippling along, getting stronger. The message is out that if you're going to be old, now is the time. For the mature adult to fail to take advantage of the challenges and opportunities of this unparalleled period in history is to be blind to one of the biggest movements of the century, a movement that may yet surpass the women's movement in its effect on society. What is happening?

More of them. Society is faced with the phenomenon of the largest mass in its population being middle-aged and older men and women. We no longer live in a dominant youth culture. Older adults now represent more than 12 percent of the population of all Americans and should make up close to 17 or 18 percent of the population by the year 2020 (Gerber et al, *Lifetrends*).

James Ellor, professor of human services at Chicago's National College of Education, has found that in any given American community, church attendance will include about 10 percent more elderly than the community at large. Thus, if a certain town has the national average of 11 to 12 percent over sixty-five, its churches will have about 21 to 22 percent elderly, or possibly even more in retirement communities (*Christianity Today*, Nov. 6, 1987).

Living longer. Not only are there more elderly, but they are also living longer. In 1900 life expectancy was 47.3. By 1950 it had risen to 68. In 1985 it was 74.7. More people survive childhood, more women survive childbirth, more people survive illnesses because of better medical care, better food, and modern medical practices. Diseases, such as pneumonia, which were once sure killers of the old, are now defeated by antibiotics (Gerber et al, *Lifetrends*).

Feeling younger. Consider this: Though society is getting older, the old are getting younger not only in appearance and energy levels, but also in attitude toward life. One man retired in 1967 at the age of seventy from his occupation as a merchant. He had worked hard keeping his small business going. He had done every task from sweeping the floor to shoveling coal for the furnace, from ordering groceries to carrying out sacks of flour and sugar on his back for his customers. He was tired, physically as well as mentally. He wanted to rest, but he never expected to rest for another twenty-one years, a rest which grew less meaningful with each day. He had been programmed to get old, not to get older. Today's older adult enters the retirement period ready for a change, eager to find new challenges.

More varieties. Everyone over sixty to sixty-five used to be dumped into one category—"over-the-hill." This typecasting is no longer possible. Those over fifty-five to sixty now divide into at least three groups with the young-old, or active old (up to about age seventy-four) in one category, a middle group that is slowing down (seventy-five to eighty-four), and a third group, referred to as the frail-old or dependent elderly (over eighty-five). But even these categories are not nailed down. All older adults do not have the same needs. They vary in gender, educational level, values and lifestyle, finances, and occupational status. Each older person is an individual, yet older people share certain characteristics, which will be discussed in future chapters.

This new group of older people is the first to have many years alone without children, although it is not uncommon for children to move back home because of financial difficulties, health reasons, or marital problems. They are also the first group to fall into what is now known as the sandwich generation—having the responsibility of caring for children and elderly parents at the same time.

Better informed. They are privileged to be the first group of older people to have a wide variety of publications prepared especially for them. In 1973 there was one publication available for the older reader. By 1977 it had grown to seven, and by 1985 to sixty. In 1988 the number was 200—and growing. Older people are one of the best informed groups about what lies ahead, the resources available to help them meet specific needs, and general information about aging.

They represent the first group to benefit from extensive research done on the process of aging. Scientists are acknowledging that aging is a process, not a radical shift from one life stage to another. This process varies within individuals and within parts of the body. Researchers have yet to come up with one single cause of aging. The two major theories according to the National Institute on Aging are (1) wear and tear. Like a car, the body simply wears out over the years, and the repair process loses its effectiveness. The rate of repair is less than the rate of damage. (2) Programmed senescence. Aging is part of human development, like childhood, adolescence, middle-adulthood. Life spans are genetically encoded in our cells. The genetic clock finally quits.

More widely traveled. Check with any travel agent to learn what age group purchased the most tickets. People over fifty buy more than 75 percent of tickets sold for vacation travel on United States carriers (Gerber et al, *Lifetrends*). Travel, both domestic and overseas, for short or long periods of time, has become an accepted way of life for many older adults.

CHANGE IS TAKING PLACE IN THE OLDER ADULT'S ROLE

In previous ages the older adults were transmitters of wisdom, culture, and tradition. Old people were guardians of the values of honor, honesty, integrity, and respectability. Older people provided continuity within the society. In primitive societies nothing of the past survived unless old people remembered it. The passing on of folklore, family stories, genealogies, vocational skills, how to take care of the sick, and how to conduct religious rites and celebrations depended on them. They were treated with respect and honor because of their wisdom and experience. In agricultural societies, where there was always some work they could do, such as grind the grain, mend clothes, or rock the cradle, they were never made to feel useless.

In time, writing displaced old people, and computers displaced them even more. Many older people's knowledge is obsolete and they lack the scientific and technological knowledge and skills to compete in the modern business and professional world. Acquiring new technological training seems terrifying. Some would rather retire than learn to use a computer or a fax machine.

Everyone grows older. A Gary Larson "Far Side" cartoon shows a truck marked OLD AGE running over an older man, leaving him lying on the street with two broad tire stripes across his back. Another old man watches what has just happened, and mutters, "Sooner or later, it gets you every time." Across his back also run two broad stripes.

Moving into the teen years is scary. In the cartoon strip, "For Better or Worse," the fifteen-year-old son says, "My voice cracks a lot, and I get sort of, you know, depressed. My knees ache, I'm always hungry, and my skin is starting to look like someone with cleats ran over it. And all the time our parents keep saying, 'Enjoy being a teenager.'"

Moving into old age is also scary. The older adult also says, "My voice cracks a lot and I get sort of, you know, depressed. Sometimes I'm lonely. My knees ache. I go to sleep at the oddest times. And my hands look like someone splashed brown ink over them. And the children say, 'Enjoy your old age—these are the golden years.'"

Negative images of old age have been perpetuated through literature for centuries. Chaucer's "Wife of Bath" adores life and in her older years falls in love and marries the young Jenkin, the sight of whose legs at her fifth husband's funeral had aroused her. Shakespeare, for all his superior intellect and literary skills, influenced many a school child forced to memorize his "seven stages of man," which describes the old man as limping onto the last stage in his "second childhood and mere oblivion, sans teeth, sans eyes, sans taste, sans everything." In *Hamlet*, Polonius is portrayed as a bungling old fool. King Lear is the father in his dotage who makes poor judgments with regard to his three daughters. In Marlowe's *Faust*, Faust gives up his hope of heaven for twenty-four years of restored youth.

A strong message to the older person is that "there is no place for you in our society." This occurs not because the aging have no place, but because society has not only "declared their place off-limits, we also suggest again and again that it is a non-place," writes Urban T. Holmes in *Ministry with the Aging.*

We cannot deny that people will age or that one may become one of the frail or dependent old. No one can assume that he or she will always be able to take care of him or herself. At some point children may have to become the caretaker. No one can assume that the packaging of his or her body will not change. Human bodies deteriorate. Eyesight dims, hearing fades, taste buds grow dull, skin wrinkles, mobility decreases.

"Old" messages have finally gotten through when you do thoughtfully what you once did instinctively. Instead of racing up the stairs, you grab the railing. You sit down to

pull on pants or hose. You allow extra time to get somewhere. You are aware something has happened.

In retirement, older adults tend to think of spending
their time in two broad categories. For the majority it
means leisure that comes earlier and for a longer time than
for the elderly of previous generations. On the other hand,
for a large minority, aging is decidedly a loss of strength,
opportunity, friends, family, finances, independence, and
meaning. It signifies becoming functionless and being
forced to enter what seems to them the "dangling modifier"
stage of life. They have nothing to relate to. Yet there is a
third option.

AGING IS GOD'S PLAN

Church leaders in the forefront of the aging movement
do not deny the reality of aging, but assert that aging is part
of God's plan. Aging does not necessarily mean moving
into a vacuum. It can be the culmination of life, a continued
time of inner growth. The apostle Paul wrote: "So we do
not lose heart. Though our outer nature is wasting away,
our inner nature is being renewed every day" (2 Cor. 4:16,
RSV). But to gain strength from Paul's words requires the
older adult to affirm boldly that continued inner growth is
possible.

Rabbi Abraham J. Heschel writes that such bold affirmation is handicapped by clinging to the dogmatic belief
that human beings can't change. He says that we conceive
of the inner life as a closed system, "as an automatic, uni-
linear, irreversible process which cannot be altered, and of
old age as a stage of stagnation into which a person enters
with his habits, follies, prejudices. To be good to the old is
to cater to their prejudices and shortcomings."

The church community can change such shortsighted
thinking by offering a better understanding of aging that
brings together faith and the daily experiences of an older
person. Preparation for growing old must begin long
before the time when health, family, finances, and friends
may diminish, long before the period normally considered

"old." It should include spiritual and theological preparation, particularly regarding a clearer knowledge of who God is and how to find courage to face life's tough final questions. To grow older challenges the individual to see life as a whole and to use these insights to live with courage, grace, meaning, and hope.

Elbert C. Cole, one of the leaders in the movement to see aging as God's plan, says, "Older adults must see themselves not just as people being maintained but as God's people with a vision of God's life for them and in turn become contributors of life."

The church must lead in this movement to provide clearer and better guidelines for growing older. It must clearly identify the resources available and not wait for government regulations to determine what will happen to the elderly. It is called to march to the tune of a different drummer by showing that aging means continued contribution to the community of faith as one is able. Sometimes it means simply being, as in the case of the dependent elderly. That may be all that God asks. But each older person needs to be assured of that.

Evelyn Eaton and James Whitehead write, "If the dominant institutions of the culture exclude . . . the aged, and if the value institu-tions—the churches, education, the arts— remain mute the elderly are left alone in the task of discerning the meaning of growing old" (*Christian Life Patterns*). This book is an effort to encourage discussion among all age groups within the faith community.

NEW TASKS FOR THE OLDER ADULT

We have twenty years of grace, said Maggie Kuhn, originator of the Gray Panthers, in 1977. She warned that if society didn't learn how to make old age a meaningful period of life, we would not survive. Heschel affirms that one ought to enter old age "the way one enters the senior year at a university, in exciting anticipation of . . . the summing-up and consummation." The goal is never to keep older adults busy, but to remind them that every "moment is an opportunity for greatness." Old age is not the glory departed.

What are some of the new tasks for the older adult in the next decades?

1. *To give old age a richer and more positive public meaning.* To restore a positive image to growing older will mean destroying the myths of aging and fighting ageism. Dread of old age lies deep in our society, partly because we derive our image of aging mostly from the media. News about the elderly is often about their poverty, illnesses, abuse, neglect, lack of involvement and productivity, senility, and inertia. If any large minority considered inferior or marginal by the dominant culture (African-Americans, Hispanics, women, singles, elderly) understands that their supposed inferiority is not because of who they are but because of an identity thrust upon them, the battle is half won.

2. *To reshape moral and ethical values.* Elizabeth Welch in *Learning to Be 85* challenges the older adult to become more aggressive in reshaping the moral quality of society. The most pressing issues of the upcoming decades will be moral ones, she writes. Older adults have the privilege and opportunity to add their voice to influence moral/ethical issues in many areas. It is not yet their turn to be silent.

3. *To bring a new approach to consumerism.* According to Ken Dychtwald and Joe Flower in *Age Wave*, the older generation is becoming a highly desirable market. Americans over fifty, who represent only 25 percent of the total U.S. population, now have a combined annual personal income of over $800 billion and control 70 percent of the total net worth of U.S. households. Members of the fifty-plus population own 80 percent of all money in U.S. savings-and-loan institutions, purchase 43 percent of all new domestic cars and 48 percent of all luxury cars, spend more money on travel and recreation than any other age group, eat out an average of three times a week, watch television more than any other age group, account for 40 percent of total consumer demand. Older consumers, however, are most interested in purchasing products or services insofar as they create a desirable experience and make the buyers feel secure

and comfortable. Money is power. What influence can the mature Christian have upon the use of scarce resources?

4. *To influence medical ethics.* Medical progress affects every age group. Much new research is contributing to a better understanding of the aging process and accompanying health problems. "Elder senility," once thought to be a result of aging, and much feared, has now been traced to Alzheimer's disease. In this decade a new and special relationship has developed between the older adult and the health care system, covering many aspects, not least of which is the increasing cost of illness care and the ethical and financial dimensions of long-term care as it affects clients and health care providers. Older people can bring about needed change by accepting that death is not a medical failure and by asserting that the older person, weak in body, spirit, and mind, unable to recognize and to respond, is still a creature made in the image of God.

5. *To strengthen family life.* An interviewer asked an old man: "Did you do anything when you were younger to take care of yourself in your old age?" The old man replied, "Yes, I had children."

Society has no precedent for the shape of the family as it involves the older adult in the future. Large numbers of children will not be part of this future family. The American family is basically a two-generation family, incapable of absorbing the increasing number of elderly. Extended families promise to be multigenerational, top-heavy with graying heads, widely scattered, with a scarcity of younger relatives but including merged families, step families, renesting of older children, and the development of a new matriarchy because of the many women who will have raised their children alone.

Who provides intimacy and support to the older adult in these new social networks? Looking after aging parents is a difficult task for the caregiver, most often a daughter, who must balance her own career with the new task. Where will the church plug in?

6. *To accept death and dying as part of the life cycle.* The

older adult must be the one to bring the topic of death and dying back into open discussion from under its covers. Urban Holmes writes that the present assumption is that if we know the physiology and psychology of death, death no longer is a problem. Such thinking reflects "our one-dimensional, disenchanted emotionally retarded culture's blindness to both mystery and the God who is the final cause . . . of death."

7. *To help the church be the church.* The body of Christ makes no distinction between races and classes. The time has come to see churches with many older members not as dying churches but as different churches. Elbert C. Cole states that churches die not because of older members, but because the needs of these adults are not met. All believers are the church, regardless of age. The church must be the extended family for older adults and take them into the inner circle of information and intimacy, not leave them on the periphery. Programming must be as extensive and vigorous for them as for youth groups.

Because older adults have learned to live with fears, to stand change, to overcome difficulties, to love, to sacrifice, and to accept life, they can make the ground firm under the feet of younger members by sharing their experiences and wisdom, especially about marriage and facing hardships. Young people, middle-aged people, older people, need to know that old age is not all frightening or sad, ugly or nonproductive—or even dull. The church can give them opportunity to glimpse the wisdom, joy, and steadiness of faith that resides in older believers.

Is there a distinct spirituality that belongs to the older person? Paul Ricoeur speaks of the Christian life as having three stages, which may or may not coincide with biological aging. In the first stage, which he labels the first naiveté, Christians believe that they've got the world by the tail, God is on their side and will protect them from danger and answer all their prayers. When these same people encounter the realities of the human condition, the stage of disillusionment may set in. They are forced to confront pain, suffering, betrayal, illness, and death. They may question their faith in God and become cynical.

But there is a third stage, which Ricoeur calls the period of second naiveté, when faith in God is restored, and believers relate to God not as blessing-machine, but as one who sees them through difficult circumstances. They believe in God because God is God. A new quiet confidence replaces the disillusionment. They are able to deal with unpleasant realities of life with or without evidence of God's activity on their behalf. They can affirm God's unconditional love and place in their lives. Though other sources of value have become unsure, faith in God gives them a calm peace. The elderly's contribution to spirituality is to bring their measure of confident trust and spirit of grace to the body of Christ. Older believers are the only ones who can teach the next generation that the Christ-way works at every stage of life.

8. *To bring a creative approach to life.* The failure of older adults to create for the first time or to continue to produce is more often attributed to a loss of psychic energy than to a loss of physical energy. They speak of lacking drive, incentive, of suffering from a failure of nerve. The development of the interior life of the intellect, memory, imagination, and creativity no longer is a challenge, or even a possibility. They see themselves as caught in an age-bind, unable to accept that a human being can continue to create in the latter phases of life.

The challenge to older adults is to continue creating—to make the word become flesh in poetry, music, writing, art, and crafts—but, in particular, to continue creating one's own life. What will help larger numbers of this age group to develop a new mind-set in which they face life, not turn away from it, and ask the big questions of life through their work and life? Jenny Joseph's popular poem, "When I am an old woman," states that when she is old she will "wear purple with a red hat which doesn't go" and "sit down on the pavement when I'm tired" and "gobble up samples in shops and press alarm bells . . . and make up for the sobriety of my youth." But such ego-transcending behavior requires practice. Can the church encourage its older members to "wear red with purple" earlier in life?

"We have to make age work for us; we can't treat it as the enemy," writes Elizabeth Welch. "To fail to utilize these untapped resources is to have a stagnant, static and unproductive Age of Gerontocracy." This book invites you to become part of the process of making age work in the community of faith. The challenges raised in this chapter become the focus of the next twelve chapters.

TO THINK AND TALK ABOUT

1. What is your dominant image of the older generation? Are you looking forward to being older than you are now?

2. Who are the older persons in your world? Does your awareness of aging come from personal experience or from the culture and the media?

3. What specific role do the elderly play in your congregation? What changes have you seen in the role of the older adult in your community? in your church?

4. What particular challenges face the older adult? Where have you seen older people change in their attitudes toward life?

Christians lean heavily on insights gained from psychology and sociology to face the declining years. Yet the Old Testament has more than 250 passages concerned with old age, extending over a thousand years and reflecting changing historical situations and sometimes different cultural influences, writes Rolf Knierem (Ministry with Aging). *Bringing together this evidence offers interesting and challenging new understandings about what it meant to be old in biblical times.*

CHAPTER 2

WHAT THE BIBLE TELLS US ABOUT GROWING OLDER

Katie Funk Wiebe

What was considered a long life in the Old Testament? We catch glimpses of antediluvians who attained eight and nine hundred years. Age span decreased with the generations. The Hebrew language has the word *heled* for "span, time, duration of life" (Ps. 39:4; 89:47), which means the total age of a person, young or old, at the time of death (Matt. 6:27). In Genesis 6:3 the life span is given as 120 years; later, the psalmist speaks of it as seventy years (90:10).

Growing old and being old were integral to a blessed and fulfilled life in biblical times. The role of the elderly was somewhat unambiguous, the last phase of a life cycle that God in his sovereignty and wisdom affirmed and directed. The aged had a high social status, for they represented the link between the past and the future. They lived with their families, occupied a central and privileged position in the household even if they became weak and unable to work. They were not isolated from the community, but continued to function according to their potential and ability. To see children and grandchildren grow up was a special blessing (see Job 42:16; Prov. 13:22; 17:6; Ruth 4:15; 2 Tim. 1:5; 3:15). An overview of some passages offers general principles applicable even today.

1. *Older people are to be respected for their wisdom and goodness.* Our present society has received a heritage, transmitted largely through the Old Testament, of honoring the elderly, although some would say this heritage is disappearing. "Show respect for old people and honor them" (Lev. 19:32a, TEV). "We admire the strength of youth and respect the gray hair of age" (Prov. 20:29, TEV) could be interpreted to mean that people replaced admiration for the physical power of youth with respect for the wisdom of the elderly. "Wisdom is with the aged, and understanding in length of days," said the writer of Job (12:12, RSV). Pharaoh respected the aged Jacob when he and his family came into his Egyptian court at Joseph's request (Gen. 47:9). David died "in a good old age, full of days, riches, and honor" (1 Chron. 29:28).

The elderly were perceived to have wisdom because of their accumulated knowledge and experience, which had developed into a tradition of mature judgment (Matt. 15:2). Wisdom in the elderly was to be respected because it had stood the test of time. Elihu, the fourth friend to visit Job in his distress, excused himself for not having spoken sooner because he was young and the others were old. "Age should speak; advanced years should teach wisdom" (Job 32: 6,7, NIV), he offered.

The ancients recognized that wisdom came from the fear of the Lord, acknowledgment of one's own insufficiency, and meditation on the law—not from having lived many years. Yet long life seems to have accompanied the seeker of wisdom: "Long life is in her [wisdom's] right hand; in her left hand are riches and honor" (Prov. 3:16, RSV). Only during social anarchy do the young rise up against the old, wrote the prophet Isaiah (3:5). If King Rehoboam at his coronation had followed the advice of his aged counselors, "the old men that stood before Solomon his father" (1 Kings

12:6), he would not have lost half his kingdom. So it is not age itself but the wisdom and righteous living that accompanies long life that is to be honored.

In the New Testament, the apostle Paul exhorts Timothy not to rebuke an older man harshly, but to treat him as if he were his own father and older women as mothers (1 Tim. 5:1,2). Peter admonishes young men, "in the same way be submissive to those who are older" (1 Peter 5:5, NIV). Respect included caring for the elderly. Paul admonishes Timothy to make sure that older widows are cared for (1 Tim. 5:4).

2. *Obedience to God's word is rewarded with long life.* That long life is a reward for obedience to God is a troubling statement to modern readers of the Bible. The writer of Proverbs states outright: "Do not forget my teaching, but keep my commands in your heart, for they will prolong your life many years and bring you prosperity" (Prov. 3:1,2, NIV). Job evidently believed that a long life was the reward for right living, yet he was puzzled that the wicked lived on, "growing old and increasing in power" and seeing their families and establishments prosper (Job 21).

God promised the young King Solomon that if he obeyed God's statutes and commands as David had done, he would be rewarded with a long life (1 Kings 3:14). This promise is reiterated numerous times in wisdom literature: Long life is promised to the one who guards his tongue and speaks the truth (Ps. 34:12); for receiving a father's sayings (Prov. 4:1,10); for keeping instruction (Prov. 10:17); for careful speech (Prov. 13:1,3); for exercising humility and fear of the Lord (Prov. 22:4,6); for hating covetousness (Prov. 28:16). Long life as a tangible reward for obeying God creates difficulties for modern believers when it is obvious that God awards long life, like rain, to both the just and the unjust. What then is the connection between obedience to the commandment to honor parents and long life, the "first commandment with a promise—that it may go well with you and that you may enjoy long life on the earth" (Eph. 6:2, NIV)?

Old Testament worshipers believed in a system of rewards for righteous living and punishments for disobedience fulfilled in this life. Job struggled intensely with this doctrine of retribution and challenged its underlying assumption because he saw himself as righteous yet suffering unjustly. Without a well-defined belief in the afterlife and hope for a continuing existence after death, the Israelite worshiper needed to settle accounts with God, at least to some extent, in the present. Long life was desired because it meant a longer time to praise God (Ps. 6:5; 30:9; 115:17) and a longer time to enjoy God's blessings. The Hebrews' hope of long life was not just a crass balancing of accounts with God but a recognition of the privilege of being in covenant with God for a longer time.

The fifth commandment ("Honor your father and your mother," Exod. 20:12; Eph. 6:1,2) was given by God to protect the family. It is one of ten commandments directed primarily to adults. Mature persons, not children, are commanded not to murder, not to commit adultery, and not to covet their neighbor's wife. The fifth commandment is therefore an admonition, not primarily to small children, but to adult children, to honor older parents.

In the Abrahamic covenant God had promised Abraham land, which his descendants would own and live in. Abraham entered that land (Canaan), raised a son there (Isaac), who had two sons (Jacob and Esau). Jacob and his wives had twelve sons. Then one day, out of jealousy, the ten adult brothers in this family sold the eleventh, younger brother, Joseph, to some Egyptians. They put a selfish concern for themselves ahead of their concern for their brother. The Israelites followed Joseph into Egypt to avoid a famine and eventually lost the land God had promised them. Their descendants, slaves in Egypt, lost their close identity with the Abrahamic covenant. In the wilderness at Sinai, at the border to the new land of Canaan, in this fifth commandment, God was warning the Israelites that the land could be lost again, writes Walter Brueggeman. It reminded the Israelites that if they honored their fathers and mothers, who had witnessed God's deliverance from Egyptian bondage, they would retain the land and their lives. Dishonor of parents broke the covenant relationship. God knew the Israelites would be tempted to forget the Exodus. If they forgot the great miracle God had done for their parents and loved the land too much, people would lose their value and they would lose both land and people. If they honored people, particularly their parents, they would retain a proper perspective of the land and retain both it and their lives. The Israelites' ability to survive as a people in the land for a long time (as opposed to a long life), as a covenant community, depended on their relationships within the family in which they acknowledged the God of their parents as well as their relationship to God.

Rabbi Abraham Heschel writes that the real bond between two generations is not a blood relationship but the insights the family members share, "the appreciation they have in common, the moment of inner experience in which they meet." The place where worth of people over land is established and nurtured is in the home and this continues into old age. The end of respect for parents by their children marks the beginning of the destruction of the home because respect for God's commandments must be preceded by respect for earthly wisdom and authority. Honor of parents and respect for the elderly leads to stability of the family and of society rather than guaranteeing long life to the individual. Some faithful live long, some do not; all have a responsibility to praise God now and to trust in the future resurrection.

3. *Old age is a time of continued service and fruit bearing.* The psalmist sang, the righteous "will still bear fruit in old age. They will stay fresh and green, proclaiming, 'The Lord is upright; he is my Rock'" (Ps. 92:14, NIV). Someone has said there is too much work in the kingdom of God to release anyone to old age. Everyone is needed to the very end in some capacity, even if only to be.

One of the most beautiful Old Testament stories of continued vigor in old age is that of the eighty-five-year-old

Caleb who came to Joshua after the conquest of Canaan with the request, "Now give me this hill country that the Lord promised me" (Josh. 14:12, NIV). He was strong, he had vision, he had hope and courage. He wanted to die climbing. When the theologian Karl Barth reached the age of eighty, he wrote another elderly theologian: "It is wonderful to feel hilarious joy—even an old tree!" Barth was referring to 2 Corinthians 9:7 where the word *cheerful* ought to be rendered *hilarious*. Barth knew, even in old age, that he could still give "prodigally and thrillingly" of his best for the world to read, as he interpreted for this generation the wondrous works of God (George A.F. Knight, *Psalms, Daily Study Bible*).

What were the tasks of the elderly? A frequent term in the Old Testament is the word *elder*, which generally refers to senior tribesmen who performed tasks of local government and justice through the biblical period (Exod. 18:13-17; 24:1-11; Num. 11:16-30; Judg. 21:16-24; 1 Sam. 8:1-9). These were not necessarily older men, although old men functioned as advisors, or wise men, in the assembly. Second Samuel 14:2 and 20:16 also speak of "wise women," although it is not clear whether they were wise individuals or prophets.

In the Old Testament old people praised God (Ps. 92:14). They had the special task to tell the next generation what God had done in the life of the Israelites (Ps. 71:18; 78:3-7).

The old were challenged to keep their minds open, because then the Lord would pour his Spirit upon all people. "Your sons and daughters will prophesy, your old men will dream dreams, your young men will see visions (Joel 2:28).

Elders in the New Testament were either important Jewish leaders (Matt. 15:2; Mark 14:43; Luke 7:3; Acts 4:8), or leaders in the emerging Christian churches (Acts 14:23; 15:2; 21:18, Titus 1:5; James 5:14). *Elder* can also mean simply an elderly person (Titus 1:5; 2:1-5; 1 Tim. 5:9-10, 17).

In the early Christian church, old men labored in the spiritual upbuilding of others in word and doctrine (Titus 1:5; Heb. 11:2; 1 Peter 5:5). An order of elderly widows was recognized for good works (1 Tim. 5:9-10). In Titus 2:1-5 older women were to instruct younger women in the ways of God. The older men were to learn to be "temperate, worthy of respect, self-controlled, and sound in faith, in love and in endurance" (NIV).

4. *Old age is a time to confront one's basic humanity.* Old age is the time to recognize that God is the giver of life and also the taker of life. Some of the most touching words in the Old Testament are the psalmist's plea: "Do not cast me away when I am old, do not forsake me when my strength is gone" (Ps. 71:9, NIV). In very old age life is stripped to its essentials, and in the words of Arthur Becker (*Ministry with Older Persons*), we are once again "brought face to face with the fundamental realities of human existence, which, in our affluent, plastic world, we have spent a lifetime glossing over." These human essentials, which older adults must face, adds Douglas John Hall in *God and Human Suffering* are "our essential loneliness as humans" and "our freedom to be choosing persons instead of instinctual animals." In old age we also confront "our fundamental limits as creatures, not the Creator, depending always upon God and others to sustain us."

Church elder B.B. Janz of Coaldale, Alberta, was a man of great spiritual gifts and many responsibilities. Toward the end of his days, when his health was failing, his biographer recounts that he resented the loneliness of old age, the limitations of his weakening condition, and the awareness that the church, which he had loved and served many years, was moving ahead without him. Like Job of old, he felt he had "stayed in God's paths" and had "not refused his commandments." Could not God spare him this last suffering when his former labors, successes, and honors were falling away?

Old age in the Old Testament is often accompanied by limitations. "The days of our years are threescore years and ten; and if by reason of strength they be fourscore years, yet is their strength labor and sorrow" (Ps. 90:10, KJV). The prophet Isaiah compares a human being to grass, whose

glory departs when the grass withers and the flowers fall
(40:6-8). Moses was unusual for an older person. When, at
the age of 120, he viewed the Promised Land from afar,
"his eye was not dim, nor his natural force abated" (Deut.
34:7, RSV). But others—Isaac, Jacob, Eli (1 Sam. 3:2), the
prophet Ahijah (1 Kings 14:4)—were blind or practically so
in old age. Proverbs 31:30 (NIV) speaks of the loss of beauty
in an older person.

In one of the most poetically beautiful passages in the
Old Testament the Preacher in Ecclesiastes 12 compares an
aging person to a great house in decline. The "evil days"
have arrived. The former glory is gone and the house is now
under threat. The writer offers this touching example of a
frail elderly person as an incentive to youth to begin their
faith journey when young. It can get tough later on in life.

Detail by detail, using poetic imagery, the Preacher distances
himself from the painful subject matter of a human
being losing strength and joy. Sensitivity to stimuli has been
dulled, so pleasure in life is lacking (12:1). In youth the
weather may look clear and bright, but clouds never stay
away forever; like rain, tears always return.

"Keepers" may refer to arms and hands that protect the
body as guards do a palace. The legs (or the shoulders), like
the supporting pillars of an old house, stoop. Loss of
strength, and particularly eyesight (12:3) is mentioned also
elsewhere (Gen. 48:10; Deut. 34:7; 1 Kings 14:4; Ps. 71:9). The
grinders, or teeth, stop chewing because they are too few.

The doors, or ears, are closed because they are deaf; it
could also mean that hospitality has ended. Conversation is
low key because the voice has become weak, or it may mean
that eating is less noisy because the person eats only soft
food. The older person finds sleeping late difficult. Any
small noise disturbs (12:4).

Older persons are frequently afraid of heights or of
being jostled in the streets and falling. In old age, hair turns
white, like the pale almond blossoms that contrast with the
darker trees around. The usual image of a grasshopper is of
an agile insect, hopping about vigorously. The older person

is like a dry, shriveled insect dragging itself along. Nothing stimulates taste or sexual desire (12:5).

In David's time, eighty-year-old Barzillai told the king who had requested him to come with him, "I am now eighty years old. Can I tell the difference between what is good and what is not? Can your servant taste what he eats and drinks? Can I still hear the voices of men and women singers? Why should your servant be an added burden to my lord the king?" (2 Sam. 19:35, NIV). Such feelings are not unusual among the frail elderly.

Youth are urged to consider the place of God in life before life ends, before the silver cord suspending the golden lamp bowl, from which the wick draws its oil (symbol of life), the pitcher at the spring, or the wheel at the well (also a symbol of life) are broken (12:6).

Verse 8 reiterates the beginning words. Everything—wisdom, power, foolishness, work, social injustice, property, youth, and age—which seems so important when young, is meaningless in old age, a chasing after the wind, an illusion. Each in itself offers nothing to provide answers to questions about the meaning of life. Pessimistic? No. Painful self-awareness of the realities of old age.

But there is another facet to this grim side of old age. The older generation is not immune to sin. The men who clamored for Lot to bring out his daughters for them to have sex with included young and old (Gen. 19:4). The older generation in Exodus 3 refused to trust, grew weary, cynical, lost a sense of expectancy, and became calloused, explains Brueggeman. They experienced doubt, discouragement and feared risking even with God's promise of provision. When the Israelites were about to enter the Promised Land, the spies returned, two with positive reports, and ten with stories of giants and grim forebodings. And because the older generation with the exception of Caleb and Joshua refused to risk, they did not enter into the Promised Land.

5. *Old age is a time of breakthroughs of God's faithfulness and grace.* The biblical picture of old age does not end with

darkness. Whether a person is young or old doesn't matter: God continues to work in a person's life. God has promised to be with us to the end: "Never will I leave you; never will I forsake you" (Heb. 13:5, NIV). God affirms the life cycle. "Even to your old age and gray hairs I am he, I am he who will sustain you. I have made you and I will carry you; I will sustain you . . . and I will rescue you" (Isa. 46:4).

As Mary and Joseph were leaving the temple after presenting their newborn son, the aged Simeon stopped them. He recognized their son as the Messiah and, taking the child Jesus into his arms, praised God, for his eyes had seen God's salvation (Luke 2:29,30). The elderly Anna likewise praised God for the child as the "redemption of Jerusalem." God crowned her years of service by letting her see the Messiah in person.

The elderly Abraham and Sarah, after many years of barrenness, were given the announcement by three heavenly beings that Sarah would bear a son though she was "worn out" and her "master" was old (Gen. 18:10). God broke through to Elizabeth and Zechariah, granting them a child of miraculous grace in their old age, for which they were thankful rather than ashamed.

The prophet Zechariah writes that in the new kingdom "old men will dream dreams," a statement reaffirmed by Peter in Acts 2:14-21. Old age does not mean the end of glory.

6. *Old age is a time to bless others and let go.* The last years for many elderly in the Bible was a time of grace and hope. It represented a conscious completion of one's life, a recognition that it could not be changed and one's task must be turned over to the care of the next generation. After having mentored the younger Elisha, the prophet Elijah, before he left this world, passed on his cloak and his task to the younger man (2 Kings 2:11).

Before he died, in one grand moment, the patriarch Jacob gathered his sons around him, blessed each one according to his special traits and died (Gen. 49:28). Granting a final oral blessing was a tradition of those times. The reality of God was still very apparent to this old man with a highly colorful past. In those days parents lived on in their children; therefore having children eased the pain of death because they would carry on in the spirit of the elders. But not everyone lets go easily. Even today people cling to ideas, congregations, institutions and agencies, whose future they will not share, as if they own them. At death they have no choice but to bequeath these responsibilities to a younger generation. Now like then, in biblical times, some older people need encouragement to let go, say good-bye and move on. Although David was very old, he continued to reign, creating conditions ripe for political chaos, until his wife Bathsheba urged him to keep his promise to make his son Solomon king after him and prevent Adonijah from taking control of the country (1 Kings 1:11-14).

The apostle Paul utters a challenging statement to all facing the final transition into glory: "I have fought the good fight, I have finished the race, I have kept the faith. Now there is in store for me the crown of righteousness" (2 Tim. 4:7, NIV).

To THINK AND TALK ABOUT

1. Do people today consider long life a blessing? Should we pray for long life?

2. What are the specific tasks of older adults in your congregation? Would it help to have "emeritus" positions on church boards?

3. List suggestions for younger people by which they can win the respect of older people. List suggestions for older people by which they can win the respect of younger people.

4. What makes it hard to let go of positions and roles one has been involved with? How can this transition be made easier?

5. What helps you to face the reality of decreasing health and strength in old age?

The population of the United States is becoming older. In 1900 only 4 percent of the population was considered aged, while today about 12 percent is in that category. By 2010, sociologists estimate this rate will increase to 14 percent. Older people today face a number of problems related to finances, housing, and health. The aging of America also has a number of implications for society involving family structures, political influence, and economics. For a variety of reasons the elderly in the United States today have little to do with religious leadership as opposed to the older persons in more traditional societies. Sociologist Dwight E. Roth invites a closer look at these concerns.

CHAPTER 3

THE AGING REVOLUTION: ITS EFFECTS ON THE OLDER PERSON AND ON SOCIETY

Dwight E. Roth

The twentieth century has been a time of significant technological change. Someone born before the turn of the century and still alive today has seen the development of the automobile, electricity, radio, television, the jet age, and the computer. At present we are in the midst of a revolution in medical technology. These radical changes in medicine, along with the fact that fewer babies are being born, have brought about a social revolution in the United States related to a particular age group: the elderly constitute a larger percentage of the total population than at any other time in our history.

The United States Bureau of Census projects that by the year 2000, the United States will have almost 35 million people over 65 (13 percent of the population) as compared to 3 million in 1900 (4 percent). Older adults over the age of sixty-five now represent more than 12 percent of the population of all Americans and should make up close to 17 percent of the population (51 million) by the year 2020 (American Association of Retired Persons). They will number over 39 million in 2010 (14 percent). This increase in the number and percentage of older persons is affecting society in a variety of ways.

THE MEANING OF AGE

Aging is the process that begins at conception and continues throughout one's life until death. All societies recognize at least three age groupings: childhood, adulthood, and the elderly. The definition of each age group varies from one culture to another.

A functional definition of aging

In most premodern societies, age is defined in a functional way. For example, some Native American tribes traditionally have seen the male adult's role as hunter, warrior, or food-gatherer. When the man becomes elderly, his functions may change to include that of counselor, healer, or teacher.

Older persons in such societies are seen as the most important and respected persons for at least two reasons. First, they are the storehouses of knowledge necessary for the survival and well-being of that way of life. Also, because they are relatively close to death, they are seen as being closer to the supernatural. Generally, where age is defined functionally, older persons have positive, meaningful social roles.

In some premodern societies, the elderly were left to die in the wilderness or buried alive. From our modern perspective, such a practice seems cruel. However, in societies such as traditional Samoa, the elderly who were buried alive gained prestige for themselves and their family. In such cases, the elderly often looked forward to being "released from the fetters of age" and entry into a joyful afterlife, writes Lowell D. Holmes (*Other Cultures, Elder Years*).

A chronological definition of aging

In the modern world, age is defined chronologically, that is, in terms of number of years lived. For example, our society assumes that adulthood starts at age twenty-five and old age at sixty-five. These well-defined starting ages reflect our modern emphasis on the precise and efficient use of time. We live out our lives on time-based schedules. We go to work from 8 to 5, we eat at 7, 12, and 6. The idea that a person becomes old at sixty-five is arbitrary. Why not say a person is old at sixty-eight or seventy-four?

The age of sixty-five to denote old age was first used in 1883 by the German government to establish a social security system for the elderly. The United States government adopted this definition for being elderly in establishing the 1935 Social Security Act.

A major problem with using a specific number of years to define being old is that different people age in different ways. Charles Zastrow writes that the elderly are "an extremely diverse group of people, spanning a 30-35 year age range." Because of the large age range, people of sixty-five are substantially different from people of ninety-five (*Introduction to Social Welfare*).

As a response to the problems associated with using age sixty-five to define being elderly, sociologists divide older adults into three groups: the young old (sixty-five to seventy-four), the middle old (seventy-five to eighty-four), and the old old (eighty-five and over). If, as noted above, a functional definition of old age generally gives the older person positive roles, a chronological definition, as seen in the modern, Western world, leaves many of them without meaningful identity.

This loss of identity is especially true for men who obtain a significant part of their identity from their former career(s). Loss of meaning may lead to despondency and suicide. Indeed, while older adults represent about 12 percent of the U.S. population, they comprise 25 percent of the people who take their own life, writes Zastrow. The highest rate of suicide within the elderly as a group is among white males, for whom retiring from a prestigious career is a crucial change.

Traditionally most women have received a significant part of their identity from their domestic work. Thus, women are less likely to face identity problems related to retirement. Their role as worker within the home in their older years does not vary much from what it was before that time. As women increasingly find careers outside the home, they may possibly face the identity problems traditionally faced by males.

PROBLEMS FACING THE AGED

Finances. There are two contrasting viewpoints about the financial well-being of the aged in the United States. One position says older persons for the most part are in good financial shape compared to the rest of society. This argument suggests that older Americans are now more affluent than any previous generation of their age group in our history. A contrasting argument suggests that older persons' wealth is exaggerated and some of them have great economic need. Both positions have truth in them.

According to Philip R. Popple, one fourth of older persons have enough money to live in expensive surroundings, buy luxury items, and travel extensively. The majority are homeowners and thus do not have mortgage payments (*Social Work and Social Welfare in American Society*).

On the other hand, according to Alex Thio, most older persons live on fixed incomes and are more likely to face huge medical bills (*Sociology*). The majority of them live on a lower standard of living than they did before retirement. When the typical older person leaves the work force, he or she usually experiences a one-third to one-half drop in income (Shepard, *Sociology*).

Few of today's elderly made enough money during their working years to save large sums of money for retirement. Investment plans, such as Individual Retirement Accounts, were not available during most of their working years. As a result, Social Security is the only source of income for about 80 percent of the elderly. This income in many cases is helped by governmental programs such as Medicare, food stamps, tax exemptions, and Supplementary Securities Income for the poor elderly. The federal government states that about 12 percent of people sixty-five and over live in poverty. Another 8 percent are near the poverty line. The poverty rate for the U.S. population generally is 13 percent. Certain groups of elderly are especially hard hit by poverty: Native Americans (65 percent), African Americans (31.5 percent), Hispanic (23.9 percent), and older women, who account for three fourths of the elderly poor (Shepard and Popple).

Being female and a person of color is economic double jeopardy. In *Aging and the Individual and Society*, Georgia M. Barrow writes about the "feminization of poverty." She states that the poverty of the elderly is "a problem of women and minority groups." During the last twenty years poverty rates for single older females have not dropped as sharply as they have for single men or married couples in the same age category (Karen C. Holden, "Poverty and Living Arrangements Among Older Women," *Journal of Gerontology*).

Joseph Heffernan suggests that a myth exists that older adults need less income to meet their needs. Their need to purchase food, clothing, shelter, recreation, transportation, and so forth does not decline with age. If their financial needs are unmet, the elderly may experience feelings of inadequacy and loss of self-esteem (*Social Work and Social Welfare*).

Housing. In the United States, many people think a majority of the older population live in nursing homes. The fact is that only 5 percent of people sixty-five and over live in such institutions. But, it is estimated that 25 percent of those eighty and over will at some point spend time in a nursing home. Currently, there are about 16,380 nursing homes in the country, and the average cost of being a resident in one of these settings is about $30,000 a year.

The quality of these homes ranges from excellent to unsatisfactory. The better homes provide comfortable, caring environments for the elderly to live in. Social isolation, patient abuse, and over-sedation of residents have been reported in some of the unsatisfactory ones. The majority of nursing homes in the nation are private for-profit institutions. Private non-profit homes are often sponsored by religious groups.

The 95 percent of older persons who do not live in nursing homes reside in various settings. While the majority of them are homeowners, many live in substandard housing because they cannot afford needed repairs. The percentage of older persons living in substandard housing is greater than for any other age group. Sociologists estimate that 30 percent suffer problems related to poor housing, with weatherproofing and exposed electrical wiring the most common ones. The urban older person is especially vulnerable to crime, while the rural poor older person may lack easy access to needed services located in distant cities.

Government-funded housing is available for individuals below a certain income level, but it is difficult to obtain because of the high demand. When available, such housing is sometimes unattractive and impersonal (Heffernan, *Social Work and Social Welfare*). Good to excellent housing is available to those aged who can afford it. Higher quality housing often includes medical and social services, leisure activities, and a variety of other amenities.

Housing communes that provide family-type living are rare. In this setting, individuals share living costs and experience social interaction with a variety of individuals.

What is the present situation regarding the elderly and housing?

* 70 percent of elderly males are married and live with their wives.

* About 65 percent of the females in the same age group live alone since women tend to outlive their husbands.

* Of the nearly 8 million older people living alone, 80 percent are women. Whatever problems elderly have in living alone, such as loneliness, fear, poor nutrition, are experienced primarily by women (Uhlenberg, *The Elderly as Pioneers*).

* Only a small minority of the elderly live with their children.

* In spite of the belief that children abandon their aged parents, many elderly report frequent contact with family members. Studies suggest that Mexican-American and African-American older persons interact more often with their children than do white elderly (Popple).

Physical and mental health. A majority of people sixty-five and older say that their health is good. Still, physical illness is more common among this age group than among younger people. The physical changes that accompany aging as well as social and psychological stress related to age are some reasons older persons have health problems. Yet only about 5 percent of them are so ill that they have to be bedridden. Men are more likely than women to develop a serious illness, and minority groups and the poor more likely to become seriously ill than white middle-class groups (Zastrow).

The most frequent health problems the older person faces are arthritis, hypertension, and hearing impairment. Other chronic diseases more likely to be found in older persons are heart disease, cancer, and arteriosclerosis. The most common form of emotional problems among the older person is depression, with a higher percentage of suicide among them than among younger people, as noted earlier.

The idea that most elderly are senile, have memory loss, and are overly dependent on caregivers is incorrect. What is labeled as senility is often believed to be a permanent condition, when, in fact, more often than not, it can be reversed with medication and/or counseling. About 3 percent of the elderly suffer from Alzheimer's disease, an incurable brain disease, the symptoms of which include memory loss and disorientation (Thio).

AGING OF AMERICA: IMPLICATIONS FOR SOCIETY

Ken Dychtwald and Joe Flower, in *Age Wave*, reflect upon the social changes that will accompany the growing number of older people in our society. According to these authors, the changes amount to a "social revolution" within the United States. Some significant aspects of this revolution are related to the family, political forces, social security benefits, and medical costs.

Family. Regarding the family, Dychtwald and Flower suggest that throughout the twentieth century the American family has been child-focused. This traditional focus is evolving into a new family form to serve the needs of older persons. Ten percent of the elderly have children who are also considered old. The average American, for the first time in history, has more living parents that he or she has children. Of older persons who need care today, 80 percent receive this care from family members.

A recent development is the "sandwich generation," which refers to persons responsible for the care of both their aging parents and their children. The most typical types of care these adult children give their parents is related to housekeeping, financial advice and management, transportation, and companionship. This added task can be physically and emotionally draining for the caregiver, most often a daughter. Programs are developing to give emotional support to the sandwich generation, such as day care for the elderly and self-help groups, such as Children with Aging Parents.

Political effects. Dychtwald and Flower suggest that political activism of the aged is "unrivaled by any population segment or special interest group." Some politically powerful interest groups are the American Association of Retired Persons (AARP), the National Retired Teachers Association (NRTA), and the Gray Panthers. Significant legislative victories won for older people in the last ten years include the Social Security reform of 1983, which rescued this system from bankruptcy, and, in 1986, the elimination of mandatory retirement at any age for most workers.

As the political power of older persons increases during the next decades, the tension between them and younger persons could lead to conflict. The Social Security system is one possible area of serious conflict. A key issue here is the number of workers who pay taxes into the Social Security fund per recipient of benefits (support ratio). In 1935, the first year of Social Security benefits, this ratio was forty workers per one recipient; in 1950 it was seventeen to one. In 1990 this ratio was 3.4 workers per recipient, and it is estimated that the ratio will be 1.78 per recipient in 2010 (Dychtwald).

If Social Security continues to pay benefits at the present rate, workers will have to bear increasing financial responsibility for the system. Lee Smith suggests that if there is no change in the system, workers twenty years from now will be taxed 40 percent of their wages for Social Security (*The Elderly: Opposing Viewpoints*). The potential for conflict is obvious: workers will not want to bear that financial responsibility, and older persons will not want a decrease in their benefits.

Those individuals who are eligible for Social Security benefits are also eligible for Medicare, a program designed by the U.S. government to help persons sixty-five and over with hospital and other medical costs. However, both Medicare and Medicaid (covering people who are poor and/or not eligible for Social Security) leave millions of older persons with huge medical bills to be paid out of their pockets, or with no medical treatment.

Some social critics suggest that every U.S. citizen should have full medical coverage paid with tax dollars. On the other hand, others, such as Richard D. Lamm, former governor of Colorado, suggest that the elderly, especially the very ill, should not have a right to such coverage. They hold that one reason for the astronomical rise of medical costs over the last decade has been the treatment of the chronically ill elderly. Why should the young have to help pay for this medical treatment with their tax dollars? Why not use this money on the millions of children in our country who receive little or no medical treatment due to financial reasons (*The Elderly: Opposing Viewpoints*).

Aging and religion. As with society at large, almost all North American Christianity has been youth-oriented throughout most of this century, especially in the last forty years. Many congregations today have youth ministers, but few have ministers for the aged. Many congregations have a young people's organization, but few have organizations for older persons. The board of elders of many congregations is usually a group of middle-aged persons. Older people in most churches in this decade do not have leadership roles. On the other hand, older people in premodern societies from the Amish to traditional African tribes serve as religious leaders. The Amish often have leaders in their twenties or thirties serving alongside older leaders to combine the energy of youth and the wisdom of age. When one Amish minister in Yoder, Kansas, died in 1989, he was ninety-two years old and had served as a minister for seventy-five years!

Paul M. Miller, in discussing the role and function of older persons in the *Gospel Herald*, asks the following questions related to the church:

1. Where is there, anywhere in our contemporary society, anything of the biblical and early church conviction that the aged are a special gift to God's pilgrim people?

2. Where is the belief that the aged are stewards of the accumulated wisdom of yesterday, which . . . they are commanded to speak?

3. What happened to the feeling that the aged had the power to bless and give a benediction to sons and daughters (Gen. 49:33)?

4. When did God tell the people to stop cherishing the teachings of their elders or to stop gathering a wisdom literature? When and how will the prophetic hope be realized that the visions of youth will be in dialogue with the memories, wisdom, and dreams of the aged (Joel 2:28)?

Many older persons respond to these questions by saying, "We have done enough church work. We want to relax and let younger people do the work." Some may not want to get involved because of a common myth that they are "has-been's, over-the-hill, not relevant" to a rapidly changing world. Given Miller's ideas, for an older adult to draw back is to shirk one's duties.

To reestablish the teaching role of older persons in the community of faith would redefine their identity in a positive way. By reflecting on the past, older persons provide younger people with a sense of continuity in a rapidly changing world. And then they would be doing what humanity generally has expected of its older citizens for thousands of years.

TO THINK AND TALK ABOUT

1. How do you define the elderly in your congregation, chronologically or functionally? What proof can you give?

2. Take another look at Paul M. Miller's four questions (p. 36). How would you answer them?

3. What is your congregation doing to enable older persons to share their wisdom with younger members?

4. How do you respond to an older person who says, "I've done my share of church work. I want to relax. Now it's your turn"?

5. If you have some "sandwich generation" persons in your congregation, have them share their experiences. What help are they getting? From whom are they getting it?

6. Some children used to support their aging parents. If the "support ratio" regarding Social Security becomes excessive, would children be ready to support their parents again?

The media have contributed to subtle and not so subtle stereotypes of and ambivalent attitudes toward aging. The media endorse two main images of older adults: one, a group of people who have been rejected by a society that traditionally values people by their work. Consequently, the older adults are people with problems, or a problem class. They are people without a future. That is one view.

On the other hand, the media portray older people as living in the golden years, with much leisure and many resources at their disposal.

Neither image is correct. Older people come in as many varieties as Campbell's soups. They have age in common, but beyond that they have individual interests, skills, hopes, and dreams. Katie Funk Wiebe takes a look at the way language and movies and television influences this image-building.

CHAPTER 4

MEDIA AND THE MATURE ADULT: THE IMAGE AND THE REALITY

Katie Funk Wiebe

In 1970 *Time* magazine carried an article titled "The Old in the Country of the Young." A photograph shows a row of four old, slightly eccentric-looking women, garlanded with costume jewelry, clutching purses to their bodies. They are sitting on a park bench, vacantly watching the passing parade of life.

The accompanying article describes the "poignant trend" in society of the gradual devaluation of older people with implications of segregation and alienation. It compares the elderly and the young: both are largely unemployed, introspective and often depressed; the bodies and psyches of both groups are in the process of change; both are heavy users of drugs. Both the old and the young are obsessed with time, but they figure it differently, one from their passage since birth, the other backwards from their death day.

A 1992 article in *Fortune* magazine is titled "The Tyranny of America's Old." A picture shows a group of older persons—Power Riders, or "geezers in gear" (leather jackets and helmets)—laughing hilariously, about to roar off on their motorcycles.

The accompanying article describes the way the "greedy elderly" are unintentionally forcing the nation to shortchange its young. It hints at a major generational war. Words like *old, poor, frail,* and *deserving* used in the 1970 article are replaced by terms like *pensioners on the golf course, geriatric avarice, elderly dandies,* and *golden oldies.*

Both articles and pictures distort the image of the elderly. Twenty years ago the elderly were not all weak, powerless, frail, and dependent any more than today the elderly are all wealthy, indifferent to the needs of others, and aiming for control. Obviously, society's image of the older person is in flux.

THE FORMER STEREOTYPE OF THE OLDER ADULT

Until the early 1980s the prevailing image of the elderly was as a group of lonely, decrepit couch potatoes, whose main activity was watching television or retelling boring old stories. They were viewed as inactive, asexual, docile, bored, typically alone, abandoned by family, highly susceptible to fraud, and unjustly treated. People thought of them as mostly living in institutions, disengaged from responsibility.

The greatest myth was probably that they were a homogeneous group. Roy L. Walford, in *Maximum Life Span* (Avon, 1984), states that society saw the elderly as "a vast swarm of the slowly dying, the undead, wrinkled and wheedling, a sorry lot and nobody's idea of anything to be desired. In an age of obsolescence, like old broken things, they joined the items to be tossed out." Young was considered beautiful; old was ugly.

Images are powerful. Older people meekly accepted the myth of obsolescence, ugliness, and uselessness and withdrew, some becoming apathetic and indolent. Yet, as Walford points out, young people deprived of social roles, as in times of massive unemployment, adopt the same attitudes of apathy and laziness (*Maximum Life Span*).

Dr. Robert N. Butler argued in 1975 in his Pulitzer prize-winning analysis of being old in contemporary America, *Why Survive?*, that a profound prejudice existed against the elderly that extended beyond the fear of growing old. He labeled this systematic stereotyping and discrimination of people because they are old as "ageism." "Aging is the neglected stepchild of the life cycle," he said.

A 1975 Louis Harris study of attitudes towards the old supported Butler's statement. It determined that regardless of income, education, sex, race, or age, Americans do not consider the aged very active, alert, efficient, or contented. "Media coverage of the elderly poor, the elderly sick, the elderly institutionalized, and the elderly unemployed or retired may be protecting or reinforcing the distorted stereotypes of the elderly," stated the study. Older people portrayed in television and in commercials lacked the full range of human emotions and weaknesses expressed by young actors, and they came through as flat, uninteresting characters.

Instead of looking forward to the elder years, people faced them with fear and ignorance because they were vulnerable to stereotypical thinking. This negative image of the elderly prevailed until the early 1980s and has not been completely erased.

WHAT FACTORS CONTRIBUTE TO THIS IMAGE OF OLDER PEOPLE?

The role of language

A primary tool used to establish attitudes toward any object or person, whether it is breakfast cereal or the presidency, is language. Thomas Szasz writes in *The Second Sin* that "in the animal kingdom, the rule is, eat or be eaten; in

the human kingdom, define or be defined." In ordinary
life, the struggle is not for guns but for words, writes Szasz.
"Whoever first defines the situation is the victor; his adver-
sary, the victim." The media earlier defined the elderly as
poor, sick, and withdrawn. Today the media are defining
the elderly as rich, energetic, and selfish. The image that
adheres will be the victor and all society the loser.

Defining, or naming, is always an act with conse-
quences. African-Americans in an earlier era (and sometimes even today) were defined as inferior human beings.
They were called *niggers* and *Negroes*, words burdened with
negative connotations. Once blacks understood that to
allow others to define them was to remain forever inferior,
they refused these demeaning labels and gave themselves
new names. In a nationwide societal movement, the old
derogatory terms were abolished as black pride grew.
Today the term *nigger* is a vicious obscenity, and only the
ignorant and prejudiced use it.

Ancient Cicero could write that "old age is the consummation of life, just as of a play." When modern society
denies that such a positive view reflects reality, that negative attitude is mirrored in our language and transferred
into actions. Prejudice toward the elderly is the result.

Society has no existing label for an older adult person
that is acceptable to this growing group of people. For
decades *old* has been a four-letter word and the resulting
harm is great. A fifty-eight-year-old executive said, "If some-
body handed me a magazine that was clearly labeled for the
elderly, I would have to read it inside of *Playboy* or *Esquire*."
A difficulty in writing this book was finding terminology to
describe the target audience without offense. Advertisers
have found that to market products for the "old" person is
to lose out. People will not buy a product specifically
labeled for "old people."

The editor of *Modern Maturity* once suggested that the
appearance of his periodical should say, "This could be any
magazine." Since 1980 the magazine has carried no ads for
dentures, hemorrhoid treatments, products dealing with

incontinence, or wheelchairs (although it does accept ads for three-wheeled scooters). No headline may contain the word *pain*. The tone of advertisements must be upbeat (*Lifetrends*).

Why the refusal to use the word *old*?

The reason is the connotations that the word *old* carries. An older edition of *Roget's Thesaurus* (1941) reveals that synonyms for *old* for that period were *antiquated, rococo, after-age, obsolete, fusty, moth-eaten, out-of-date, out-of-fashion, stale, behind the age, behind the times, passé, gone out, outworn, run out, disused, senile, time-worn, crumbling, deteriorated, secondhand*. No word in this list of synonyms carries the positive meaning of integrity, dignity, wisdom, worthwhileness, and experience.

During the same era the reader could choose from the following synonyms to describe an old woman: *crochety, dame, gammer, old girl, nag, crone, bag, bat, biddy, drab, trot, witch*.

Synonyms for an old man were only slightly better: *gaffer, graybeard, patriarch, duffer, geezer, grandfather, old boy, veteran*. A check with *Roget's Thesaurus* even as late as 1976 defines old-womanish as *choosy, fastidious, finicky, fussy, old-maidish, particular, persnickety, picky, squeamish*.

Who wants to be called "old" when the images of that stage in life are mostly negative? But the stereotyping goes on.

Journalists are criticized for identifying older women as grandmothers, or grandmotherly types, even though they don't identify men as grandfathers. Referring to someone as a "septuagenarian" or "octogenarian" when the age of other people in the news story is omitted is also considered a form of ageism.

Writers and editors frown on the use of *girl* or *boy* when applied to a task done by a female of any age, as in hat check girl, camera girl, career girl, water boy, office boy. This usage ("I'll get one of the girls to make a copy for you," when the "girl" is fifty-five years of age) has overtones of immaturity and dependence and carries a patronizing tone. During slave times and thereafter, minority men resented deeply being called "boy" when they were adult men. One phrase using "boy" that survives with a functional connotation is "good old boy network," meaning an exclusive informal system of networking used by business and political men. Attempts have been made to introduce "good old girls network" but without much success.

Some older persons think that for too long this generation has allowed itself to be defined by euphemisms like *senior citizen* and *golden ager*. It is time to resist. The word is out that it's okay to be older. The baby boomers who will be hitting fifty about 1996 will enter the later years with a different image of what they want their old age to be like than those who grew up during the Depression. They will refuse to be labeled *crocks, old coot, little old ladies in tennis shoes* or *elderly dandies* and *wealthy geezers*.

Maggie Kuhn of the Grey Panthers states: "We are not 'senior citizens' or 'golden agers.' We are the elders, the experienced ones; we are maturing, growing adults responsible for the survival of our society." Elizabeth Welch, in *Learning to Be 85*, speaks of "elderhood" and the Age of Gerontocracy. A fresh wind is ruffling gray heads.

Despite rooted-in-cement stereotypes, new words are moving in fast. The newly retired speak of themselves as the *young-old, the older American,* or *the mature adult.* Terms like *retirement centers* are disappearing as are *old folks home* and *home for the aged.* We will hear people use more terms like *active adult community, mature adult,* or *older adult.*

Even dictionaries reflect this gradual evolution of language. *Random House Dictionary* has three terms for this older group: *Old* for someone who has lived long, *aged* for someone advanced in years with infirmities, and *elderly* for those somewhat old, but usually retaining "the mellowness, satisfactions and joys of previous age."

THE ROLE OF MOVIES AND TELEVISION IN STEREOTYPING

The image of the elderly on television and in movies is also changing from the highly stereotypical one of the elderly as not fully functioning human beings of thirty years ago to glimpses of them as vigorous and involved with life.

On Golden Pond, Fried Green Tomatoes, and *Driving Miss Daisy* are just three examples. Lucrative markets among the older adults are part of the reason.

Real older people were missing on television in the 1950s, '60s, '70s. Active life ended at middle age on the television screen, write the authors of *Lifetrends*. Older people were depicted as "cute, comical, pathetic, nearly always incidental to the plot," and/or played by character actors. They had no serious place in anyone's life, including their own.

Old age was something to defeat. An Oil of Olay ad of this earlier period when the in-phrase was to "grow old gracefully," showed a thirtyish model saying, "I don't intend to grow old gracefully. I intend to fight it every step of the way."

The 1950s and l960s focused on children's programing like "Little Rascals" and "Leave It to Beaver." Older characters tended to be "powerless, befuddled, inflexible and feeble, with no sex appeal," adds Sally Steenland in *Prime Time Woman: An Analysis of Older Women on Entertainment TV.*

Messages in television commercials and periodical advertising were almost always delivered by young actors and actresses, with a particular bias against older women. From 1960 to 1979 only 2 percent of adults in advertisements were over sixty at a time when 21 percent of the population was over sixty. Four percent of women in ads were over forty while 57 percent of the population of women was over forty *(Age Wave)*. Advertising used older women to promote hemorrhoids, arthritis remedies, diuretics, and products related to menopause.

In the late l970s and early l980s media treatment of the elderly continued to follow the earlier model—older adults were generally ignored or stereotyped in portrayal. Nancy K. Schlossberg summarizes in *Forum* (Phi Kappa Phi Journal) the image of the elderly during this period:

* the elderly were underrepresented

* older men outnumbered older women three to one

* proportionately fewer older characters were "good" and proportionately more older characters were "bad," especially older men

* when the success of a character was measured, more older women were unsuccessful than successful

* elderly women were disproportionately portrayed as victims, and as persons in poor health.

The media portrayed older women as "self-effacing helpmates to their aging spouses, quaint grandmothers, pathetic widows, or eccentric 'biddy' spinsters. With the coming of menopause in their late forties or early fifties, their most important job, bearing children, had ended. Publicly they were held sexless, no longer desirable to men" (*Lifetrends*). Alex Comfort (*A Good Life*) writes that in 1976 media catered little to seniors because their financing objectives did not include them, but suggested change was coming. The change began in the early to mid-eighties with older men in leading shows—Brian Keith ("Hardcastle and McCormack"), Jack Warren ("Crazy Like a Fox"), John Forsythe ("Dynasty"), Edward Woodward ("The Equalizer").

The most severe negative stereotype was nearly out of date in the late 1970s and 80s. Even Wendy's "Where's the beef?" ad with Clara Peller insulted some older people because it imaged older people as "silly, cranky, funny-looking." The truck ad with the oddly-dressed older woman shouting, "Don't you buy no ugly truck," was resisted for the same reason.

If the elderly were shown as poor and powerless before, in the late 1980s it was fashionable to flip the coin and depict older adults as "universally affluent and politically unstoppable" and that there were too many of them, or as "lovable grandparents." Women were shown as powerful, creative, appealing, and affluent, writes Steenland. On shows like "Dallas," "Falcon Crest," and "Dynasty," 25 percent of the women are millionaires owning their own businesses. The Pepsi generation is now fifteen to seventy-five, instead of fifteen to twenty-five.

Yet despite some gains, women are still the losers. Dalma Heyn, columnist for *Mademoiselle* and former executive editor of *McCalls*, wrote in 1987 that adulthood for women stops somewhere around thirty-five to forty in the media. Editors delete quotes from older women in stories and excise age from photographs. Female readers at age sixty have no "realistic image models" in these magazines. They compare themselves to some retouched face smiling back at them and come away the loser. Feminist Gloria Steinem stated "an over-50 Dan Rather is regarded as the young replacement for Walter Cronkite while Barbara Walters is treated as a miracle of longevity."

The popular television situation comedy "Golden Girls" shows attractive older women dealing with real-life problems like widowhood, sexuality, desertion for a younger woman, children's marriages, grandchildren, economics. They hold real-life jobs—but Mary Cassata and Barbara Irwin report that in a survey of viewers they learned that some viewers found the characters "overdrawn and predictable—three immature, single women and their 80-year-old mascot who shocks with scatological language" (*Media & Values*, Winter 1989, No. 45).

Donna Demac admires Jessica Fletcher (Angela Lansbury) of "Murder, She Wrote," but still wishes the mystery writer had a more typical family situation—a household to run, a boss, a pension to worry about, or hassles with her publisher. "If the typical image of an older woman is a Hausfrau clown, Jessica Fletcher offers another model, in which aging gracefully requires that a woman be a major success, live alone, work for no one and have little contact with the wider society" (*Media & Values*), an image that is unrealistic for most women.

In the 1990s, networks fishing for more profitable markets debate seriously whether to appeal to the older audience or to a more youthful one when they withdraw a program series.

NEW MYTHS ABOUT THE OLDER ADULT

Not all the myths regarding the elderly have been dispelled. New ones are always developing. The new image of senior wealth has come about by advertisers focusing on the healthy and affluent among them and excluding the poor and sick.

This new image may make the image too rosy. Senior poverty is still more prevalent than poverty among other adults. One out of eight older Americans is surviving below the official poverty line. Many older people scrape by on only their Social Security. Sociologists agree that poverty is still concentrated among older single women living alone.

Dan Rather (CBS) reported in February 1992 of the increasing age discrimination in the job market because older workers are informed they can't work as well in the marketplace as younger ones. In 1991 he reported a 12 percent increase in age discrimination cases before the courts. Older people were being forced out of their jobs in favor of younger people.

Violations are subtle and hard to prove. "We need more young people to keep us light on our feet," said one employer. Whereas at one time a worker could rely on the company to take care of him or her in return for a lifetime of good work, this is no longer the case. Older people are losing jobs and with them pension and health benefits, possibly introducing a new group of older poor who once lived very well. Another developing myth is of a major war developing between the generations as both groups are forced to compete for scarce resources. In 1946, 30 to 40 percent of elderly parents received more than half their income from children. In 1987 a Harris Poll revealed that less than one percent did. In other words, older people are supporting themselves today while a large number were dependent on children in earlier decades. Few parents or children would want to revert to that earlier dependence of the elderly on children for financial support.

Ronald F. Pollack argues that it is not true that there are fewer workers or more dependents. "What has changed is the age of the dependents: fewer children and more grandparents. In fact, there are more workers to support the community and far fewer children to be educated, fed, clothed and nurtured" (Media & Values).

THE OLDER ADULT'S USE OF THE MEDIA

Because the elderly are harder to impress, advertisers are being forced to change their advertising directed toward this group. They may watch more television than some other group, but they have more "smarts" about products and claims. Television particularly attracts four groups: women, blacks, the poor, and the elderly. Women watch more television than men, and older people more than younger people. Social class has an inverse relationship to the amount of viewing.

A strong need exists to convince those who control the media to reflect the changing demography in their depiction of the older generation. The media need to reflect that adults of the same ages are not successively experiencing similar stages, tasks, or transitions. "Adults need to be viewed and portrayed as individuals—some of whom are healthy, some unhealthy, some sexually alive, others 'dead,' some happy, some sad, some productive, others unproductive," said one writer. We shortchange ourselves when we oversimplify what it means to grow old or accept the stereotypes presented by the media.

TO THINK AND TALK ABOUT

1. What word do you use to refer to your own age group? What words do you use to apply to others of the same age? Which words do you object to? Does society need new terminology to describe the older adult?

2. Review recent television programs or movies you have seen. How were the elderly portrayed in them? Do the same for commercials. What kind of products do older people promote?

3. If you were honest with yourself, would you think of yourself as prejudiced against the elderly? What if they were called "mature adults"?

4. Jobs and Social Security benefits are at stake in the new "generation war." How can a confrontation of serious dimensions be averted?

5. What role has the church played in stereotyping the

older adult and also the teenager? What can the church do to change this?

6. Do you want to grow old? Why or why not?

PART II

THE CHALLENGE

*T*he lions of the later years crouch at the door ready to pounce on older adults who risk stepping beyond their comfort zone. These lions come in many forms and sizes from feelings of inferiority and powerlessness to wondering how much an older person is responsible for society's needs, especially as it concerns the generation of children growing up in a troubled world. Is it time to bow out or to keep reaching for the goal?

Decision making is very much a part of growing older. In this way, this period of life resembles the period of youth. Who am I? Where am I going? Who will be going with me in this journey? What should I do? All are questions the older adult asks. What place does faith have in making decisions? And to these are added some new ones: When death is close, what choices do I make with regard to my estate, medical care, funeral arrangements, and death itself?

At the time of the division of the Promised Land, after the conquest, eighty-five-year-old Caleb made a strange request. He was one of the two spies who some forty years earlier had encouraged Joshua to move ahead and take the land. He knew the Israelites could win the battle. Now he asked Joshua, "Give me this hill country that the Lord promised me that day" (Josh. 14:12). His age did not deter him from accepting the challenge of the hill country. He wanted to die climbing. He wanted to die reaching for the goal.

Challenges are best seen as adventures in faith for which God provides wisdom and grace. But in the community of faith, the whole body joins in that adventure of making life full and rich for the older adult. Death then becomes the glorious climax to a faithful journey, with older adults as cheerleaders of life, leading the way. Their God-given task is to show church and society that faith makes a difference in the older years as they pass on wisdom, educate, model, and inspire those coming after them. To die climbing grants hope for the journey, not just for the end of the journey.

Retirement has become an institutionalized rite of passage for the older employed person. At age sixty-five or thereabouts the individual passes from the world of work to another world, not always of his or her choosing. Loss of identity is a serious concern for many older persons because of society's emphasis that identity is often determined by what one did in one's productive years rather than who one is. How does one create new roles and new values and become more aware of one's power? How can this important milestone become a more integral part of faith and church life?

CHAPTER 5

RETIREMENT: FRIEND OR FOE?

Katie Funk Wiebe

Retirement is one aspect of aging expected of people in the workplace. On a designated day, sometimes at a designated age, the worker surrenders keys and symbols of work and authority, such as uniform, nameplate or identification tag, car keys and expense account. He or she abandons schedules and regulations participated in and enjoyed, sometimes for several decades, to sever the workplace connection.

The daily routine may have been enjoyed or endured, but that is over. No longer will the retiree get ready in the morning to go to work, punch a time clock, give or receive instructions, enjoy coffee break conversation with co-workers. That life is over. This leave-taking may be followed by high moments such as dinners, awards, certificates, plaques, speeches, and well wishes to complete the formal aspect of the institution of retirement.

According to Random House Dictionary, to retire means "to withdraw, or go away or apart"—to become disengaged. Traditionally it has come to mean to move from "an active, specific and role-related identity in the community to a stage where one is relatively less active and has been retired from a specific role in the community," state Evelyn Eaton Whitehead and James D. Whitehead (*Ministry with the Aging*). A businessperson is no longer a businessperson, a teacher no longer a teacher, a computer programmer no longer a programmer. He or she is retired.

WHAT IS RETIREMENT?

Today retirement is seen as an important milestone, the reward for years of long, hard work. It is made possible because of pension plans and Social Security payments and greater affluence. "Retirement is no longer a luxury, it is now an institution," reports the United States Senate Special Committee on Aging. Until most recently it was an institution that involved mostly men. Women did not have the work history that entitled them to pensions or Social Security other than as wives of retirees, although that is changing. Though retirement is now a major predictable life event for employed persons, they respond to its various aspects differently. Some people make an easy transition into this new stage in adult life. Many farmers retire so slowly that it is only a gentle upheaval in their routine. From managing the entire operations to the point when they drive out occasionally to the farm to check the crops may take years.

Others find retirement a difficult and stressful rite of passage. Walter Cronkite, former CBS evening news anchor, believes that "broad-gauged people probably have nothing to fear from retirement." Workers know it's coming. They have seen parents and friends' parents retire with varying degrees of success. Consequently, retirement is sometimes welcomed, sometimes dreaded, sometimes blessed, sometimes cursed. It does not mean the same thing to every person.

Some anticipate retirement with joy and recognize it as a transition into a new and important stage of adult development. Some couples look forward to more time together. "It's like being in heaven and still being alive," said a seventy-three-year-old woman living in a retirement community in Florida. "I've got my ceramics and my painting. I've got a wonderful husband who I met here."

For some workers, retirement represents giving up on a grand scale. They see it as the stage signaling declining health and death. They speak of this period with resentment, depression, and anger. Horace Greeley Smith writes of retirement as humiliation: "Only those who have passed through its portals know the sense of emptiness created for the man who one day has a full schedule of things to do and on the next faces a day without a single date or appointment" (*Don't Retire from Life*).

Older single persons recognize that retirement takes them out of regular daily contact with people, a vacuum that may be difficult to fill. People with limited resources may wonder how they will manage on only Social Security benefits, unlike the wealthy who look forward to a wide range of leisure activities on a more than adequate pension plan and investments.

HISTORY OF RETIREMENT

Historically, most persons continued to work until health made work impossible. They lived alone as long as their health and financial circumstances allowed or moved in with children when the situation became impossible alone. The Amish, for example, still have a *grossdoddy* house attached to the main house or close to it, where the elderly live out their years.

Then came Social Security and pensions. The Social Security aspect of retirement grew out of social conditions in the country. Social Security began in the United States in the 1930s. One of its first goals was to get older people out of the labor force to open more jobs for the young.

Only after World War II did retirement become separated from concerns about poverty, and begin to resemble the institution we know today. Pensions were viewed as "deferred wages" instead of handouts. Retirement was promoted as "a legitimate stage of life and a good bargain for everyone." It made room for the baby boomers to move into the work force and offered older people a reward for their years of work. One sociologist states that "people learned to want retirement, and to be willing to bear economic sacrifices in order to have it."

The U.S. government paid the first retirement benefits before World War II when sixty-five was set as the age of retirement. Life expectancy in 1940 was sixty-three. Today nearly 80 percent of Americans will live to be past sixty-five (Gerber et al, *Lifetrends*).

REASONS FOR RETIREMENT

Retirement does not take place at the same time or for the same reasons for every person, nor do all retirees look forward to the same kind of life.

1. Sometimes workplace regulations stipulate retirement at a specific age, often sixty-five, although this number is creeping up. Social Security benefits at a lower rate may be applied for at the lower age of sixty-two, if desired.

2. Some people are bored with what they're doing and can't see themselves starting a new career. Or they like what they're doing but don't want to work as long and as hard as their present job requires. Or their work is physically hard and intellectually not stimulating.

3. The worker's health may begin to deteriorate, making full-time work impossible.

4. Some near-retirement workers are laid off and are never called back, forcing retirement, for they never find another job.

5. Some people are paid to take early retirement, often to reduce the work force or to hire younger or less experienced workers at lower wages/salaries.

6. Some people drop out of the work force early in order to spend time in voluntary service.

PREPARATION FOR RETIREMENT

Because of the longer period of time people today will be out of the work force, without children to care for, and because of longer life expectancy, it is important to think ahead to the retirement years. The following are some of the significant questions that need answers beforehand:

1. *When should I retire?* Some gerontologists agree that retirement is expected too early today because people are in better health and could continue to work. Most people want to decide their own time of retirement, but not all have a choice. Our society today is much more concerned about a person's age as it relates to occupation than it was a century ago. John Wesley was eighty-one when he reluctantly decided to ordain missionaries for America. His advanced age was not considered significant. Pope John XXIII was seventy-eight when he called Vatican Council II.

Creative persons work well beyond the time society says they should retire, or they apply their knowledge and creative skills to a new field or business. Church leaders, politicians, college professors, musicians, writers, editors, farmers, and other professionals tend to stay in their work as long as possible because they get enjoyment out of their work. Sophocles wrote *Oedipus Rex* in his eighties. Benjamin Franklin invented bifocals at seventy-eight. Grandma Moses painted some of her best pictures when she was in her ninth decade.

2. *How will I spend my time?* A retiree faces approximately 2,000 hours of discretionary time that was previously filled with work. Time can become an enemy or a friend. Because retirees don't really know what lies ahead, some people attach a kind of romanticism to retirement. They look forward to sleeping in, enjoying free time, having a second cup of coffee, taking time to read the paper and play golf or do hobbies. Only later do some discover they need a more structured life to maintain meaning. "What the retired need . . . isn't leisure, it's occupation," writes Alex Comfort in *A Good Age*. "Two weeks is about the ideal length of time to retire." One man said, "I got tired of sitting around, spending fifteen or more hours a day doing nothing."

The best approach is not to find something to kill time, but to make it come alive. "There is nothing more frightening and demeaning than to be ushered into the world of jig-saw puzzles, bingo and small crafts and be told, `This is your life,'" writes one retiree. Anyone planning to quit work should examine interests and skills that can be continued for several decades. For many people the joy of retirement means having the privilege of choosing their activities. Yet retirees often speak of the enormous pressure imposed by others to become involved in projects.

Continued full-time employment is an option for some. More retired persons continue to work full-time when wages rise. They drop out of the work force if they have enough income to live adequately. Receiving only Social Security benefits increases the possibility of part-time work or becoming involved in a second or even a third career.

Volunteerism is one of the main ways elders spend their time. Between 1977 and 1986 the number of Americans who did volunteer work increased from 27 per-cent to 36 percent. College graduates over fifty did more of this unpaid labor than anyone else. Another survey reports that almost 44 percent of those between ages fifty and sev-enty-four do volunteer work (Gerber et al, *Lifetrends*).

Church organizations, like Mennonite Association for Retired Persons (MARP), offer retirees challenging oppor-tunities for service that match their interests and skills in overseas or domestic mission projects. In the spring of 1992, volunteers, many of them retired craftsmen, includ-ing carpenters, plumbers, electricians, and bricklayers, once again built a house in North Newton, Kansas, that was auctioned off at the annual Mennonite Central Committee (MCC) relief sale. Proceeds went to MCC's global relief ser-vices. This type of project is duplicated in other places. At MCC sales, observers soon notice the large number of vol-unteers in the gray division.

Hospice is staffed largely with older volunteers. They can also be found in civic, health, church, educational, and political institutions. So important is volunteerism to the health of a community, that some newspapers, like the

Wichita (Kansas) *Eagle,* carry a weekly list of volunteer openings with training possibilities.

Another viable option for retirees is to return to school, part-time or full-time, for a degree or for enrichment. Elder Hostels have proven attractive to countless older persons. Many colleges offer continuing education courses for the older population and permit auditing of regular classes at no or a reduced fee. The goal of education should be self-discovery and achievement, as well as general information.

3. *How much money will I need? Where will the money come from?* The ancient thinker Cicero wrote that "old age is impossible to bear in extreme poverty, even if one is a philosopher." The older worker should engage in financial planning for retirement long before the date when the job ends. He or she should investigate resources available when compensated work is no longer an option. Some people can look forward only to Social Security, although baby boomers are being warned not to depend on it. Other workers can plan on private pensions, survivor's insurance, savings, and investments. Some will need assistance from local and federal social agencies. Does the church have a responsibility here?

4. *What are my health needs? Medical insurance needs?* Ordinary retirement today means the retiree goes on with whatever satisfied in the past, if health and income are adequate, state the authors of one study of twenty-five retirees in a Midwest plant. Older people are more conscious of their health than young people and are becoming healthier as they change lifestyle, eating, and exercise habits. Most older people are not in poor health. Only five percent of those over 65 are in nursing homes, although with increasing age that figure increases dramatically. Statistics show that older workers consistently have fewer sick days per year than younger ones.

5. *Where will I live?* When should I move if a move seems necessary? Into what kind of living arrangement? House, apartment, condominium, retirement center, with

children? How far will I be from family, church, community activities, shopping? What transportation is available?

A move is best made in consultation with family and friends. If a move is going to be made eventually, the retiree should consider making it sooner rather than later so that memories can be accumulated in the new place, whether it is a house or a room. People need the opportunity and time to do some living to develop memories in the new setting. A move to a retirement center is often made late in life, sometimes leaving the person feeling lost and lonely in the strange surroundings without familiar furniture, personal possessions and activities, and little energy to make it a place of loving memories.

6. *What is my family situation?* Some couples look forward to having more time to spend together. Others may have to learn to make adjustments to spending twenty-four hours a day together. In an oft-quoted quip, the wife of a retiree complains, "I married him for better or for worse, but not for lunch every day."

Single people, whether never-married, widowed, or divorced, and those with health problems face a different set of questions. Researchers have found that it is fairly easy to develop a pattern of life that is full of activity if there are others with whom to share. Single people frequently ask the challenging question, "Who will be with me when I am old?"

7. *What will give me identity and meaning as I grow older?* In "Death of a Salesman," Arthur Miller's play that takes place in the 1930s, the main character, Willy Loman, faces forced retirement from his job as a traveling salesman. His son Biff comments that "he never knew who he was." In life Willy never found his own identity. He always assumed the identity of the most popular salesman in his district and in the end it failed him. Some people pine away and become depressed because of lack of self-worth as a noncontributing member of society. Though society's attitude toward the elderly is changing, discriminating attitudes remain. To know oneself and develop good self-esteem are important ingredients in a good retirement because the retiree will

sooner or later confront society's attitude toward him or her as an "old" person.

If older persons had difficulty identifying themselves as middle-aged until the end of that period, they may find it even more difficult to identify themselves as old, older, or even aging. A person's attitude toward aging and identification with this age group needs clarification in retirement. It is important to ask: When I retire will I associate with other "old" people? But what if I still feel young? Does anyone ever feel old? How will I identify myself? as a retiree? by my former occupation? The identity a worker gives up is always clearer than the vague roles society assigns to retirees. Avoiding persons in the same or older age bracket is not the answer.

WOMEN AND RETIREMENT

When does an older wife's retirement come? Only when her husband dies if retirement means change, bluntly states one gerontologist. Many women not employed outside the home never actually "retire," but continue to do whatever it was they were doing before the husband retired.

The older woman is the neglected person in retirement issues. Her kind is a majority within the graying majority. She usually lives on a lower income than men. She is more dependent upon social service programs. Both widowhood and divorce are difficult for the older woman who has not experienced independent living before the loss of her husband.

Many face old age without close family members to provide social, emotional, or financial support. They are not usually the group in the center of church life. Sometimes they continue to function as heads of households with dependent spouse and/or frail older relative.

Who is the older woman? Elizabeth Welch describes her: "She may be widowed, living alone, divorced, living in an institution, or living on the street. She may be a receiver of assistance or a producer and donor of her invaluable experience as an independent, creative, resourceful, and achieving person, interested and interesting. The potential is great, both for her own self-realization and for her world" (*Learning to Be 85*). But that potential is not always recognized.

STAGES IN RETIREMENT

According to the Whiteheads, retirement is not a one-step affair like walking over the threshold of a new house. Although for some it may be a smooth transition, for most it comes in stages and has been compared to the stages that occur in any major life change. The Whiteheads identify these stages as follows:

1. Social identity is changed or removed for those whose social life and identity were wrapped up in the workplace. Rites of passage, such as retirement dinners and accompanying accolades, both protect and predict the older person, write the Whiteheads. They show respect and appreciation for what the person has accomplished in life. They protect by helping persons in transition identify and acknowledge the danger of the passage they are entering. They openly acknowledge that a new stage lies ahead with its own dangers for which there must be preparation.

2. Anxiety and disorientation. Retirement does not mean immediately having a new identity that fits like a new garment. Though some reach for this new stage in life with joy, others feel like a discarded tire, something to be shoved into a corner. For a time the retiree may mourn the death of a previous way of life and feel anxiety, ambiguity, and loss of direction before moving to the next stage. Gone is the old familiar life in the workplace among adult co-workers. Ahead lies uncertainty.

3. The ideal pattern would be to follow the second stage with inner resolution as the retiree learns to enjoy more leisure and adopts a new sense of personal value and worth apart from being socially and economically productive. The focus shifts to being rather than doing.

The Whiteheads recommend that the church, together with its elders, learn to celebrate "uselessness," because the Christian's worth before God rests not on works but on faith in God's love. Too frequently retirees receive too much

advice on how to find something to do; often they try franti-
cally to fit in every new activity. Christians are not justified
by their works. God loves us as we are. Life is a gift. A believer in Christ doesn't have to do anything to be a worthwhile
member of the community of faith (*Christian Life Patterns*).

WHAT MAY LIE AHEAD FOR THE INSTITUTION OF RETIREMENT?

1. The word *retirement* may bow out and be replaced by
reinvestment or *reengagement*. Robert N. Butler argues that
society must free itself from seeing life as three separate
periods: education, work, and retirement. They run concur-
rently and continuously. In the future, retirement, as we
know it now, will no longer exist. Instead, people will speak
of second and third careers, intergenerational education,
or even of "first retirement," "second retirement," and
"final retirement."

2. *Old* may become a disability that makes one eligible
for getting a disability pension in a low market demand for
older workers.

3. Present retirement practices will cause development
of distinct social classes among the elderly according to
retirement income. On the one hand, there will be an
increasing number of very poor elderly. On the other hand
will be the very rich, dedicated to a leisure-oriented lifestyle
that may include second homes, retirement communities,
travel, and private sheltered housing schemes. This discrep-
ancy in income and interests will become a major challenge
to the church.

4. Women will feature more largely in the discussion of
retirement. Elder baby boomer women will have their own
pensions comparable to those that male counterparts
receive and their own health care programs. Older women,
because there are more women than men, will by their presence determine the quality of life in church and society,
writes Elizabeth Welch (*Learning to Be 85*).

5. Church and society will recognize the terrible waste
of elder talents and gifts and think through how these can

be incorporated into the life and work of church and community more effectively.

TO THINK AND TALK ABOUT

1. Although retirement has been seen primarily as a marketplace event, it affects most church members in some way. How can this important milestone be brought into the celebrative life of the church? What can the church do to help people make the smooth transition into post-employment living?

2. Ask some older people to share their experiences before Social Security was instituted. How were the old supported?

3. Are hobbies a suitable substitute for work?

4. Ask some retired persons to share their experiences with retirement. Do they agree with the Whiteheads' analysis of retirement?

5. What is the obligation of the church family and the biological family to older people who do not have the means to retire adequately?

6. Talk with some persons you see as role models for retirement living, either in their own homes or in retirement centers. How did they successfully navigate this transition?

Some losses we face in life are expected, some unexpected. We expect the death of a parent, retirement, and marriage of children. We do not expect or plan for the death of a child or spouse, divorce, job loss, sickness, accident, environmental disaster, loss of friends, loss of hearing, sight, memory, mobility, maybe even a driver's license.

When an older person faces loss, what are the resources for meeting these losses in one's inner being, one's faith, one's faith community? How does one move from the breakdown of usual and comfortable patterns of living and living defensively to creative reordering and beginning again? Katie Funk Wiebe states that the task for every person, whatever his or her age, is to build a spirituality that sees loss as part of God's pattern for humanity.

CHAPTER 6

TURNING LOSSES INTO GAINS: IT'S POSSIBLE!

Katie Funk Wiebe

In *The View from Eighty*, Malcolm Cowley writes that most of the literature on the subject of the older years is written too positively because the writers are fifty and sixty. At that period in life they are looking ahead to old age and "lack genuine knowledge of the process of aging and are trying to be cheerful." He adds that they deny that growing older means loss, sometimes severe loss. And that each loss is a small death that must be dealt with.

WHAT ARE THE LOSSES?

Although everyone starts aging soon after birth, the first apparent loss in mid-life is usually a change in eyesight. You find yourself squinting, holding the book at arm's length. To your dismay the optometrist prescribes bifocals.

Next, spouse or friend gently tweaks a gray hair from your head. You knew it was there but didn't want to admit it. Add to this the awareness that your hair is thinning. One day you consciously part your hair lower and comb a lock over the growing bald spot. On occasion you notice you ask speakers to repeat their words, "What did you say?" Background noise has begun to bother you.

Mobility and agility decrease. One afternoon you decide you'd better not drive to the evening service. It's raining and glare on the wet pavement bothers your eyes. A while ago you gave up long-distance travel. Too wearying. You sense your independence is being chipped away at the edges.

Weeding the garden and climbing stairs you once leaped up two at a time become a chore. You encourage your granddaughter to practice hard at the piano; your fingers are much too stiff to make ragtime music sound like anything but a lullaby. And when you decide to go out to the garage to your workbench, you remember you gave away half your tools when you moved. And, in time, maybe even the car won't be there.

Names of people you know well slip into a black hole of forgetfulness. You know your neighbor's name has an "L" in it, but you can't retrieve the rest from your sluggish memory bank. Bible verses you were sure you would never forget elude you. You walk into the kitchen from the living room to get something, only to stand, perplexed, wondering what it was you came for. So you retrace your steps—and your thoughts—and come back for the scissors.

Wrinkles may look attractive on Ronald Reagan or Queen Elizabeth but not on you. Yesterday you caught yourself matching blood pressure and cholesterol levels with your friends. Last summer's skirt or pants have a strange fit this year. You turn away from your image reflected in store mirrors. This person with gray hair, arm flaps and dewlaps, flat breasts and jutting stomach isn't really you. The real you is someone quite different.

And then there are the embarrassing matters you hesitate to discuss even with your doctor, like decreasing sexual potency, especially devastating to men, and slight incontinence, more common in women.

As if this isn't enough, jumbled among these losses are others, much greater in intensity and scope, such as surgical removal of an organ or awareness of the development of a long-term illness. Last year you lost your spouse, this year a grandchild. You scan the obituary section of the daily paper to find out who died overnight—and their ages. They include persons from your age group—and younger. And you wonder when friends will read your obituary and what their reactions will be.

In a weak moment you let people tear huge chunks out of your self-esteem by their deprecating attitude. The salesman calls you, "Young lady." The nurse speaks down to you as if you're a child. The clerk in the shoe store looks at you pityingly when you struggle up from the low chair as awkwardly as a cow.

What is left to make you feel good about yourself? You're no longer in the work force. Your influence on others is practically nil because of the loss of daily contacts with people. You have few responsibilities. You've lost the roles of leader, worker, and helper—and sometimes parent, spouse, and friend. In time your children may have to take care of you. Friendships wither because of lack of opportunity to get together.

Opportunities to attend worship services, family reunions, and shopping trips slip from you. You make fewer trips to the bank because there isn't reason to go. When the offering is passed, people don't expect you to give as you used to. You feel anger, loneliness, sadness, and despair. The backdrop of your feelings is death.

"We start by growing old in other people's eyes, and then slowly we come to share their judgment," writes Cowley. Whereas for quite a time you may have asked yourself, "Am I old?", even denied it, now you are forced to say, "I am old." This crisis in identity happens in solitude, without much understanding and support from others.

To live is to change. Change means loss. Each loss, however small, is a separation, a death. And each death demands the hard work of mourning and pushing ahead to new life.

HOW DOES ONE DEAL WITH LOSS?

Some older people feel besieged by the losses in their lives, so much so that they conclude there is no meaning in life if they cannot work or move about freely. The Preacher in Ecclesiastes wrote about the "days of trouble." He found "no pleasure" in being old (12:1). Life for many older people becomes restrictive, hedged in at every turn by physical, social, economic, or psychological limitations. The task for every person, whatever his or her age, is to build a spirituality that sees loss as part of God's pattern for humanity. Loss can be an opportunity for growth. Each loss is a transition into another stage of life, not lesser, but different.

At one point in his life, the apostle Paul had lost his freedom through imprisonment, his reputation as an educated, influential Pharisee, and his health through persecution. Yet he wrote, "We are hard pressed on every side, but not crushed; perplexed, but not in despair, persecuted, but not abandoned, struck down, but not destroyed. For we who are alive are always being given over to death for Jesus' sake, so that his life may be revealed in our mortal body" (2 Cor. 4:8-9,11, NIV).

The besieged Paul recognized the many losses in his life, but also the opportunity to show the "all-surpassing power" of God. His words to the Corinthian church are words for any older person: "Therefore we do not lose heart. Though outwardly we are wasting away, yet inwardly we are being renewed day by day" (v. 16).

HOW CAN LOSSES BE EXCHANGED FOR GAINS?

Dealing with loss in old age has two aspects: saying good-bye to what has been (or letting go), and saying hello to (or welcoming) what lies ahead. This approach to life must begin before one is "old," for as psychologist Erik Erikson writes, "What comes later is the cumulative product of earlier stages successfully negotiated." More simply put, we become what we were, or as we are now, so we will be when we are old, only more so.

As we move through life's stages, we need to let go of the previous stage no matter how much we enjoyed it, and greet the next one lovingly, for it too has glories. We will never discover the splendors of the new age if we cling to the previous stage with the tenacity of Superglue and carry baggage from it into the next.

A teenager has to let go of adolescent attitudes and behaviors, like hanging around with the gang, to become a responsible young man or woman. Young adults have to relinquish certain freedoms to accept the privileges and responsibilities of parenthood. It doesn't work to have two sets of children in a home at the same time though the one set may be the biological parents of the other.

To refuse to move with the seasons of life limits us from entering fully into the full range of possibilities of the next stage. To enjoy the blessings of old age, the individual has to admit to being in the last quarter or third of one's life. That time has arrived. And it can be "a good age," as Dr. Alex Comfort describes it.

However, every loss, small or large, should be acknowledged as such. It is real whether it is loss of movement in a joint because of arthritis or loss of space because of a move from the spacious, comfortable, family home to a small apartment. Identify it as a loss, but also as an aspect of growing older. Mourn its passing. Share feelings about it with family and friends, and then deliberately steer into the future.

TO WHICH LOSSES SHOULD YOU SAY GOOD-BYE?

1. Say good-bye to the reality of enjoying complete independence until you die. Some older people are able to achieve independent living into their eighties and nineties, continuing to live alone, drive a car, and generally function without much assistance. Most aren't able to continue this when they get into their eighties. Accept with thankfulness the privilege of having had absolute independence, but

also acknowledge that part of God's learning is to be willing to accept help when it is needed.

The church is the body of Jesus Christ and each member is a servant ready to serve others. Even the older frail persons are members of that body. At one time they were the leaders, supporters, and caregivers. Now the time has come for someone to help them. Though accepting help is a kind of submission, it does not mean being a lesser person, or a less worthwhile person. There is a time for appropriate independence as well as appropriate dependence.

2. Say good-bye to your dreams for the previous stages of life without feelings of guilt, failure, or despondency. You will probably never be rich, never be a best-selling author, never receive the highest bid for your quilt or wood carving at the auction, but you can say, "This is my life. This is the way my life turned out, but that's okay." Erik Erikson calls the mature stage of life the period of "integrity," in which you accept your "one and only life cycle" and the givenness of it. This doesn't mean you give up and subside into the woodwork as a non-person. It simply means you accept your life, and in doing so, you affirm its meaning for others. Out of this acceptance the older person can maintain control of his or her life.

Say good-bye to bitter memories, grudges, angry episodes. Find forgiveness before God for wrong attitudes through confession. Find forgiveness of those you have hurt by making restitution and seeking reconciliation. Forgive those who have hurt you through unjust dealings and leave judgment to God. Don't carry hard feelings with you into your latter years.

3. Say good-bye to the need to control adult children, their friends, finances, education, work, and attitudes. Instead turn them into friends. You may need them later on as caregivers. Loose them to their own pursuits without passing judgment on them and let them develop in their own way, even if it's not the way you would have chosen for them.

4. Say good-bye to the world of work as you once knew it. You may have been brought up on a work ethic and

found great satisfaction in your vocation. You once went to work daily, made appointments, established work schedules, managed a farm or household, ruled a small or large company or corporation, championed important causes and projects and ideas. You also held positions in church and community. One older church leader prided himself on being repeatedly reelected to positions at church conventions. He couldn't accept that everyone is dispensable. When you are older, you need something different than "former work" to give meaning and direction to your life. Release that former life to the power of its own creating energy and create a new life.

When to say good-bye? There is no specific age. You will know when—but let it be before you sense younger workers nipping at your heels to chase you out.

TO WHAT SHOULD YOU SAY HELLO?

If it is important to say good-bye to specific aspects of life as you grow older, it is also important to welcome new opportunities and experiences in thought and action you have never had before. Spiritual growth comes at points of decision. Just as the grace of God in Christ can enter a life at any point of change, so sin can also. So decisions and movement should be made prayerfully, but deliberately.

You may have lost physical health and strength, but according to Mary Ganikos (*Counseling the Aged*), older people as a rule retain their cognitive capacities, long-term and immediate memory, personality traits, adaptability and creativity, sexuality, social awareness, willingness to nurture, appreciation for aesthetic values, and sense of well-being. These can all be translated into a meaningful life as a mature adult.

1. Say hello to finding meaning through being rather than doing. The person for whom life is meaningful makes life his or her vocation. Psychotherapist Viktor Frankl (*Man's Search for Meaning*) points out that in the concentration camp during World War II where he was imprisoned, those prisoners soon died who lived only in past memories

and experiences and no longer accepted any responsibility for life in the present.

These people lived in a difficult situation in which all decisions regarding daily activities, such as eating, clothing, work, and socializing were taken from them. They were robbed of their identity and possessions and suffered the most horrible cruelty to mind and body. Yet those who realized that even in that most difficult of all existences life expected something of them, hung on. Life became their vocation—their only vocation. They acknowledged they could choose the attitude with which to face their tenuous and tormented existence.

Some people die physically before their time; others die mentally and spiritually before their time. They outlive the goals they once set for themselves and exist on memories of who "they used to be." Life loses meaning for them. When meaning is under siege, the person, young or old, is tempted to despair.

I recall standing before a modern sculpture at a university several years ago and wondering about the meaning behind its peculiar shapes and lines. Maybe it had no meaning. Some older people stand before their lives with its strange patterns and colors and wonder also, What gives life meaning when deprivations are greater than gains?

People have various views on how to make life meaningful. For some people it is meaningful only when it is harmonious and the pattern of it is pleasant to behold—when all the pieces fit together like a 500-piece jigsaw puzzle. It is meaningful if they are successful at whatever they attempt and when work, even retirement, meshes into the pattern established by general consensus—college followed by marriage, a successful job, church and community pillar, and retirement supported by a good income with a spouse and regular trips to the Sunbelt.

I have found that some older people substitute their children's successes for the vacuum in their own lives. One older women identified herself as the "mother of the missionary to India." Others share stories of children's and grandchildren's exploits to have something to talk about.

The path to meaning lies in learning to be rather than to do. Time may streak past, but inner space, especially as one ages, should grow. Old age is the opportunity to explore one's inner world, to develop a stronger relationship with God through meditation and prayer. Many older people may live alone, yet in their solitude have found comfort in reflection and meditation.

Meaning through being comes as we learn to live with the paradoxes, absurdities, and mysteries of life that include the sorrow, pain, and suffering, the ugliness, brutality, hate, violence, and fear. We may never have all the answers to life's perplexing problems, for now "we see through a glass darkly." Many things happen in life to make one bitter and cynical, yet we can choose our attitude toward the losses we encounter. We are free to be discouraged, to be despondent, to feel imprisoned. We are also free to accept each moment as a challenge to forgive, to love, to accept God's daily grace. It is this quality of living by faith that enables an older person to step not into certainty but into the uncertainty of the unknown with the assurance of God's daily presence.

Therefore, the integrating theme of the last stage of life should be the search for the meaning of one's own life by meditation, prayer, reflection, nostalgia, storytelling—a kind of interior stocktaking to pull together the odds and ends of life. Identity for the believer comes from knowing one is a beloved son or daughter of God. That identity nurtures all of life.

Saying hello to being rather than doing means saying hello to joy, to friendship, companionship, laughter and celebration, and to new experiences. It means being open to God's presence in the people we meet, the flowers by the path, the memory of a past moment of love or of a hearty laugh with a friend.

2. Say hello to freedom from competition in the work world and wearying schedules. Forget about the alarm clock. Growing older grants the freedom from pressure to

acquire things to hang on the wall and display on tables and store on shelves and in closets. It releases one from the pressure to conform to the most recent styles in clothing.

3. Say hello to the opportunity to give back to society the lessons and resources and experience that you have harvested over a lifetime by mentoring younger persons. Erikson speaks of this process as generating, or taking responsibility for what one has created in terms of ideas, so that it will generate some more. This means having less concern for self at this point in life and more concern for what will happen to the next generation, particularly the children of our country and of Third World countries, and the needs of broader society, not just for our own children. Mentoring has a wide range of possibilities from tolerating the ideas of a younger generation to affirming and championing them even if you don't wholly agree with them.

Part of mentoring is accepting opportunities to share with others the way you've traveled—its grace, mercies, and blessings. It allows you to think of the passage from young to old as ascending, not descending. Experienced older people use life experience to enrich others' lives and to connect with the next age group. Someone has said one of the most difficult problems of our society is to invoke in others a commitment to justice and compassion, a sensitivity to needs, a sense of the holiness of God and the sacredness of life. The best way to do this is by telling stories out of your life. Everyone has a moment of insight, a memory of love, a dream of excellence, a story to tell about rising again after failure.

Yet when people talk about storytelling, they tend to think of inspiring only young people—but that is not the first and only audience. Anyone traveling on life's journey close behind you is your first audience. If you are sixty, think of those who are forty and fifty. If you are seventy and eighty, think of those who are sixty. Only those who have reached a certain age can tell the ones in the next age bracket what it means to be that many years old.

Some people fear old age, thinking that God may not come with them into the new stage of growing older—and then even older. The past had become a comfortable relationship with God. Now they ask: Do I have the promise of God's continuing help and presence when I can no longer drive and must depend on others? Only people older than they are can assure them that the faith-way works when they are alone, perhaps living in a nursing home, on a limited income. As older adults keep acknowledging that God is with them in the transitions of life, they give their listeners courage to let God enter their lives in a new way.

4. Welcome the opportunity to find an even stronger basis for your beliefs. This entails being teachable about biblical truth until death. Some older people hold themselves long and rigidly in the same theological groove. The result is the shriveled soul that shrinks back in terror when faced with rapid social and cultural change. Some older people are not prepared to meet the enemy in new shapes and sizes. They would rather not face the pain of changing their minds about life in the present. Yet theology must change with life change, with each loss or gain.

The mature adult faces life without fear even though society is changing rapidly, especially in such areas as human sexuality, abortion, pluralism, styles of worship (particularly choice of music), the role of women in church and society, poverty and social justice issues, the work ethic—an all-important cornerstone of many a person's life and considered by many as the best provider of meaning in life.

It is never too late to think through our belief system. Elders in years and experience should remain leaders in theological thought. Elton Trueblood in *Your Other Vocation* writes that the study of theology, which is concerned with the knowledge of God, is perhaps the most mature discipline in which men and women can engage. He argues that the older adult should engage in study to the end, particularly about tough questions that confront everyone:

a. How is it possible to believe in the uniqueness of the Christian revelation without at the same time, denying all validity to the teachings of the other world religions?

b. How is it possible to believe in the efficacy of intercessory prayer and yet believe that there is an objective order of natural law which makes scientific prediction of events a possibility?

c. Can we believe intelligently in both the goodness and the power of God, in view of the fact that so many innocent people suffer with such obvious injustice and without profit to themselves or others?

d. How can we believe in the evidential value of the widely reported direct experience of God when it appears that such experience is purely subjective or can be explained in psychological terms?

"I'm too old to change," say some older adults. According to gerontologists, bodies may decline with age, but spirits have the capability of soaring to new heights in later years. This is the unique and special opportunity of aging. Old age need not major in losses if transitions are seen as movement toward the culmination of a life well lived with God and humanity.

TO THINK AND TALK ABOUT

1. How can the individual establish a pattern for dealing positively with losses beginning with youth?

2. Invite some older person who has dealt positively with losses to share his or her experience with the group.

3. Read and discuss Romans 8:28-39 as it can be applied to victorious living, especially in the later years.

4. Take another look at Trueblood's questions (pp. 75-76). Do you have satisfactory answers to them?

5. How can the church encourage older people to grow in faith and inner strength?

"What does the Lord require of you?" asked the prophet Micah. The answer was "to act justly and to love mercy and to walk humbly with your God" (6:8). This comprehensive and all-embracing statement is still pertinent today to all age groups and to all areas of life, including medical ethics. Can the church truly be agents of God's grace to older adults in difficult medical decisions? It can and must. Willard S. Krabill speaks out clearly in favor of the church helping older adults make better and clearer decisions when faced with medical decisions. These should develop out of the "teaching, preaching, and guidance in the faith community."

CHAPTER 7

MEDICAL ETHICAL ISSUES FACING THE OLDER ADULT

Willard S. Krabill, M.D.

Not long ago someone close to me (in his seventies) was admitted to a medical center more than one hundred miles away for evaluation of chest pain. He had had coronary bypass surgery ten years ago and was determined, regardless of the test results, not to undergo another bypass operation. However, over the weekend, while his wife and family were briefly back in their home community, one of his physicians persuaded him to undergo surgery after all, and the procedure was underway before the family reached the hospital. The medical team performed seven bypass procedures, yet his condition rapidly deteriorated. He never got off the ventilator and so was never able to speak to his family again. He died a few days later.

This is an example of medical ethics decision making gone wrong. It illustrates how crucial clear communication is in ethical dilemmas between families and caregivers. We will never know what professional pressure caused this man to accept the bypass procedure, foregoing the opportunity to discuss it thoroughly with family and pastor. To what extent was he aware of alternatives? To what extent did he feel the support of his faith community to decline high-tech procedures?

Contrast his death with that of another aged friend thirty years earlier, before our capability of, or obsession with, resuscitative death-prolonging procedures. His condition also was deteriorating rapidly, and, at the close of my evening check on his condition, I said good-bye with the words, "I'll see you in the morning." Both of us knew "the morning" I was referring to was not on this earth. He died peacefully during the night.

Or contrast many of today's high-tech death scenarios with the death of the ancient patriarch Jacob, who, having "ended his charge to his sons, [he] drew up his feet into the bed, breathed his last, and was gathered to his people" (Gen. 49:33 NRSV). A "good death," as illustrated by this story of Jacob, is not easily achieved in today's death-denying world, but it is worth striving for.

Many people outside medical circles are intimidated when encouraged to think about medical ethics. The language of ethicists bewilders. But what we are really talking about are the "oughts" and "shoulds" of our decisions as older adults when it comes to decisions about our health and about medical treatment. All of us should develop a sense of what we ought to do and that sense should develop out of the teaching, preaching, and guidance we receive from each other in the faith community.

WHAT ASSUMPTIONS AND GIVENS SHOULD DIRECT OUR DECISIONS?

The first important given is that medical treatment decisions are ours to make. When we enter today's medical system we tend to feel a loss of control. The unequal knowledge base between ourselves and our physicians can tempt us to relinquish to physicians the decisions that we should make, based on our feelings, the meaning of our lives, our view of death, our family circumstances, our faith. Decisions regarding our medical care should not just be based on medical considerations or the availability of technology. We are the ones who control what is done to our bodies and we are entitled to all necessary information in making our decisions.

A second given is that we live in a world beyond that of biblical history. The principles are unchanging, but the dilemmas are new. The ability to keep hearts beating and lungs breathing long after personal life has ended was not a reality to the writers of Scripture. We have to search for a biblical ethic in a different world. Ours is a different ball game.

Although the Scriptures often give us no direct answers to the ethical dilemmas with which modern medicine confronts us, they do speak about principles, intentions, and beliefs that should form our character and guide our conduct. It is the purpose of this chapter to suggest some issues on which Christians might express their faith in the context of the new powers of medicine.

Third, we are dealing with true dilemmas. They cannot be solved with simple common-sense answers. There are nearly always both good and bad aspects to each choice we face. Furthermore, the choices are often not just tough; they are often tragic. Removing a feeding tube is a tragic choice, even though it may be the best available choice.

Fourth, usually no one answer fits all situations. Because the dilemmas are complex and difficult, the best choice in one situation may not be the best for another person and another situation. We must respect differing conclusions, but also be open with each other and allow the Holy Spirit to help us build consensus in dealing with medical ethics questions.

Fifth, medical treatment choices should not have to be made alone. We should be enabled to make them in community, with our families, our small group, or our congregation around us, interacting with us and supporting us.

Sixth, death is increasingly a managed event. Technology so influences death that from 70 to 75 percent of people today will die managed deaths. For more and more people, living or dying will be determined by a decision-making process on the part of someone.

Seventh, although dramatic life and death decisions get the headlines, we make most medical ethical decisions in the more mundane aspects of everyday medical care, deciding about generic drugs, visits to doctors, insistence on specialists, demands for unnecessary tests, etc.

Is the community of faith's voice needed in this medical world? It surely is. The principle at stake in many medical ethical issues for older adults is justice, and the Bible has a lot to say about justice.

Injustice is apparent when poorer people do not have access to even a decent minimum of care. Injustice is apparent in the fact that in this country we spend a thousand times more per person for health care than is available to citizens in many underdeveloped nations. Injustice is apparent in the way our health care system is much more generous to the elderly than to any other group. I believe that concern for justice in health care and for health care reform are also medical ethics issues for older adults.

WHAT LEGACY ARE WE LEAVING THE NEXT GENERATION?

The term *life cycle* is most clearly exemplified by our bodily reality. The carbon atoms that compose our physical bodies are all recycled atoms from plants and animals—from the universe that has gone before us and of which we are now a part. We are born, immediately start aging, and die. Our earthly life is a journey between birth and death during which we have opportunities to do things that will be remembered in some way. That is the legacy we pass on to those following us.

Modern medicine has forced us to think of the legacy we leave our children in a different context. We in the faith community leave the next generation the legacy of the way we have made medical decisions, following society's pattern by default rather than making faith decisions. I refer to our overall stewardship, the way in which our generation may, for our own selfish benefit, impoverish the next generations by our utilization of medical services and postponement of our dying. We are certainly doing that on the national scene (federal debt and deficit), but might also on a personal level. In our grasping for one more treatment approach against overwhelming odds, one more desperate operation, one more week of life at tremendous cost, we can, in our dying, rob the living. That kind of legacy should concern us.

Today is a time of exploding medical technology and growing numbers of older people; it is also a time of decreasing availability of public funds. The graying of America is occurring at the same time we are discovering that we can no longer "have it all." With each new medical advance we widen the gap between what we "can do," and what we "will do" (especially for those who can't pay for it). Our moral conflict in providing access to medical care thus worsens each year.

This also forecasts trouble ahead by way of intergenerational conflict. We are already hearing a growing chorus of voices that say the elderly are getting more than their fair share. Because of Medicare, many wealthy elderly have their medical bills paid while the children of poor people die from lack of care or even immunizations as state after state slashes their Medicaid budget. The federal government spends ten times as much per person on the elderly as it does on children—even though only 12 percent of the elderly live in poverty compared to 21 percent of children.

Professor Reo Christenson of Miami (Ohio) University, a political scientist, writes: "I grieve that my generation refuses to set aside its immediate self-interest and make modest sacrifices for our children, our grandchildren and our nation. That we should have become the greatest obstacle to the fiscal future of this country is both tragic and inexcusable" (*Chicago Tribune,* July 20, 1992).

WHAT INTENSITY OF TREATMENT SHOULD WE EXPECT AT THE END OF LIFE?

With what tenacity should we cling to biological existence when our personal relational journey in this life is at an end? The dilemma here is the conflict between our view of the sacredness of the life we hold in trust, and our sense of both justice and stewardship. Also at stake is our view of death and its meaning.

We live in a death-denying society. Death is seen as the end, as disaster, rather than as part of our life's journey, our "graduation." The fear of death is a major factor fueling some of the exorbitant medical costs spent to keep people alive when restoration of health or even meaningful life is impossible.

To me, some right-to-life Christians are misguided when they convey the message to the world that death must be opposed and delayed by all means and at all costs. Does the Bible really sanctify biological existence, that level of "life" that we share with the other mammals? Or does it rather hold sacred life lived in relationship—to God, to self, to one another?

Even if we believed we should preserve the physiological existence of everyone just as long as humanly and technologically possible, we could not. We do not have the resources to do that for everyone, even in this country, to say nothing of those outside our borders. We live in a world of infinite need and we have finite resources. We must set priorities, we must (and will always have to) make choices. Where, in our list of medical priorities, should we Christian older adults place desperate efforts on behalf of the dying elderly?

SHOULD AGE BE THE BASIS FOR RATIONING MEDICAL CARE?

Recognizing that we cannot give everyone all the medical care they might want or need, and recognizing the need to set priorities and limits, some have suggested that curative efforts be omitted for all persons over a certain age (e.g., age eighty-five). This is a pertinent concern when we recall that the average age of persons undergoing coronary bypass operations is steadily rising. Should we continue to fund such procedures for the frail elderly, or even heart transplants, under Medicaid, while cutting the funding for prenatal clinics, for example?

All of us know the wide variation in the vitality of persons at any given age. Some eighty-five-year-olds are both mentally and physically more vigorous than some sixty-five-year-olds. And so we recoil at the thought of using an arbitrary age cutoff to determine who gets what medical service. But if we individualize our allocation of resources, and if we make the decisions subjective, then who makes the decision, on what basis, and how do we keep the decision-makers accountable?

I believe a just society could do far better than ours is doing. I believe we could provide basic care for our children as well as a decent level of care for our frail and elderly. But we can't do it if our fixation remains on high-tech cure (rather than decent care), on a "full court press" for every individual whose body can be kept breathing.

It is more time-consuming and a great deal more difficult to decide which level of care is appropriate for aging persons. The decisions should be based on the person's needs, desire for a given level of care, and ability to benefit from it, rather than on the date of birth.

These decisions would be made more easily if we Christians voluntarily changed priorities and voluntarily restrained our demands for "everything possible." We could also acknowledge that although age alone is not the best basis on which to ration care, it is a factor, and can thus be a consideration.

IS DIVESTITURE AN ETHICAL PRACTICE?

A serious concern for many nursing home administrators is the practice of some prospective residents to divest themselves of their assets when nursing home admission becomes likely. The assets are distributed to children, or, in some cases, donated to charitable causes. Thus the persons avoid having to "spend down" their savings, and when admitted to a nursing facility, they become Medicaid-eligible quickly and their care is paid for by the government (really by all of us).

This issue calls into question our welfare and Medicaid system that invites cheating and encourages abuse. But it also calls into question our duty as honest citizens. The purchase of long-term care insurance could well be a more ethical course than many of the alternatives now being enriched by divestiture. Congregational dialogue on this issue is needed.

DOES "CAN DO" MEAN "SHOULD DO"?

The existence of technology should not obligate us to use it. There are times when we should say, "Enough is enough." Christians should be able to view their medical wants alongside community needs and interests. Christians will recognize that there are fates worse than death. They will also acknowledge that longer numbers of days of life are not necessarily the greatest good.

Some procedures and treatments are unacceptably risky and unacceptably painful and destructive. In our negotiation with physicians we need to be open, honest, questioning, and demanding of the fullest possible accounting of all the alternatives and likely outcomes. Then we, and our supporting community, have the power to decide.

ADVANCE DIRECTIVES: PLAYING GOD OR STATEMENT OF FAITH?

Our decisions about certain medical treatments can and should be communicated clearly. When the time comes that we can no longer speak, our wishes must be communicated through others who know us or to whom we have delegated the authority to make medical treatment decisions. Those who must speak for us will be helped if we have signed a living will that is a statement of our attitude and beliefs as well as our wishes regarding the use of life-sustaining technology.

Our wishes will be more likely carried out if we also name a person as our representative or proxy for medical decision making (assigning durable power of attorney for health care). Both these instruments are varieties of advance directives, and all hospitals, nursing facilities, Health Maintenance Organizations, etc., are now required by federal law to inquire whether the patient has an advance directive, and to inform him or her further about them if the patient doesn't already have one.

Some have suggested that to make an advance directive is "playing God," i.e., challenging God's sovereignty over our lives. If used by Christians, in the way and for the reasons intended, I do not believe advance directives are suicide documents. Rather, I believe they are stewardship documents, or statement-of-faith documents. The people playing God are the death-denying ones who interfere inappropriately in the completion of the dying process when all reasonable hope of recovery is gone and who, in reality, are only prolonging death, not life. I believe advance directives are a Christian responsibility (to remove a great weight from those who must someday speak for us) and provide us another opportunity to express our belief in the resurrection.

ACCEPTING DEATH, INVITING DEATH, CAUSING DEATH: IS THERE A DIFFERENCE?

An effort is being made in our society to blur the differences between allowing death and inducing death. When physician-assisted suicide was considered by the voters in Washington state in 1991, it was narrowly defeated. The issue will be appearing on the ballots of other states. Again, this is an ethical issue with which Christians must wrestle. Our voice is needed. Christian physicians and nurses must also be heard.

I can understand why some people see little difference between removing a feeding tube from a permanently unconscious individual and injecting a drug to quickly terminate biological existence. To me, however, there is a crucial difference between "getting out of the way" of a natural process and actively inducing death. It is the difference between accepting death and intending death. When it comes to public policy, that difference, to me, is critical.

Surrounding this issue is the meaning of suffering, the definition of suicide, the physician's role, the physician's view of herself or himself, and the meaning of imaging

God—these and more are the stuff on which medical ethical dialogue in the church should focus in the days ahead.

IS MUTUAL AID STILL A POSSIBILITY IN THE FAITH COMMUNITY?

A special kind of medical ethical issue for Christians is mutual aid. What does it mean to bear one another's burdens in a health care environment where uncontrolled medical costs are impoverishing many and where even rising insurance premiums are becoming unaffordable? Can we remain indifferent when our brothers and sisters are in need of care? And can we define our brothers and sisters as only those in our small group or in our congregation, ignoring those in our wider denominational family?

Mennonite Mutual Aid (MMA) was first organized to help the faith community address these concerns. But as MMA began to follow the insurance model, and had to compete with a secular insurance industry, which today avoids risk rather than spreads risk, many Mennonites abandoned MMA. Skyrocketing medical costs and insurance industry competition have forced uncomfortable choices on MMA.

Is it fair and is it honest for us to assume that our mutual aid obligations in health care can be met through a churchwide agency in which only 13 percent of us participate? Can we possibly fulfill our mutual aid responsibility through an insurance model alone?

WHAT IS THE ROLE OF PERSONAL RESPONSIBILITY?

This last ethical issue is a summary concern, but it could just as appropriately have been listed first. Many diseases that kill us today could be prevented or alleviated by living healthier lifestyles. Most of our mutual aid and insurance dilemmas have resulted from our insatiable appetite for more and newer technological fixes for diseases, many of which could have been prevented. We pay a high price for our acceptance of alcohol, tobacco, handguns, and overeating, for our nonuse of seat belts, our fast driving, our nonuse of cycle helmets, our failure to immunize poor children, etc.

Each of us and each of our congregations should be health promoters. Good stewardship and common sense demand it. Yet in our society, and unfortunately in our churches, we are focused on disease treatment far more than disease prevention, and we have it all backward.

It is not too late as older adults to adopt healthier habits. It is also part of our personal responsibility to have realistic expectations of what medicine can do for us. To reduce our demands on the system would do much to reduce costs, and thus improve access to care. Physicians are human, medical outcomes are not always good, and our attitudes should never force physicians to practice "defensive medicine," spending resources wastefully.

Taking personal responsibility means doing our part to build consensus in our congregations against over-utilization of medical services—becoming "conscientious objectors" to inappropriate medical care. It means working for a more just health care system, helping the church to be a part of shaping health care reform. It means completing advance directives. It means participating in congregational efforts to prevent AIDS, unwanted pregnancies, and sexual abuse. It means reexamination of funeral practices, another example of the way we in our dying may rob the living.

Medical ethical issues have become important concerns in our country for the past fifteen years. Debate about them will continue to intensify. Our society tends to regard these issues as political, or economic, or social. In reality they are fundamentally religious and spiritual, striking as they do at the heart of our beliefs about the meaning of life and death and the place of health in human life and purpose. Older adults face these issues with more urgency, and as we do we can lead the church into greater relevance and faithfulness.

TO THINK AND TALK ABOUT

1. What can older adults do to bring about justice in health care, especially for our children and for people of underdeveloped nations? Where does the process begin?

2. How can the church support families in making decisions when death for a frail elderly person seems imminent? What will it take to develop consensus regarding overutilization of medical services?

3. Discuss the difference between accepting death, inviting death, and causing death. What experience has your group had with such decisions?

4. Is mutual aid still an option for a highly secularized society?

5. Does your congregation have a wellness program?

6. Have a local nursing home administrator speak to you about the way divestiture affects the economy of nursing homes.

7. In what way are medical ethical issues fundamentally religious and spiritual rather than political, economic, or social?

*Does growing older mean decisions become fewer and less critical?
Not at all. Each passing year brings with it new ethical issues for
the older person to face. Life isn't over until it's over. New challenges face each older generation. American Association of Retired
Persons (AARP) president Lovalla Burgess told the 1992 conven-
tion that she "firmly believes that older people have a moral obligation to work for the benefit of all generations." Executive director
Horace B. Deets said at the same conference that AARP must be
sensitive to the needs of children and to the needs of the family. This
emphasis will include offsetting the image of the older adults as
"greedy geezers," devouring an unfair share of the federal budget.
The social issues that AARP calls older adults to confront include
poverty in their own age group, but especially among children,
health care reform, and education reform. Is the same clarion call
coming from the church to older people to face the social issues of our
time? Maynard Shelly explores some of the issues as they relate to
older persons within the community of faith. These are issues neither
older persons nor the congregation must work with alone.*

CHAPTER 8

LIFE IN THE CARING COMMUNITY: ETHICAL ISSUES FACING THE OLDER ADULT

Maynard Shelly

All of a sudden, in the spring of 1960, the unfairness
of growing older in America hit Henry A. Fast hard.
He didn't like it one bit. He had been teaching at a
college in Kansas for sixteen years. On his way to a special
faculty meeting, he began to feel troubled.

"It dawned on me," he said, "that something related to me was taking place." He was given a gift. A speech was made about him. Both seemed to say, "It was good to know you."

The shock cut deep. He was in the prime of his life. But he no longer had the job he had enjoyed so much. "I had presumably been an esteemed teacher and suddenly, in a day's time, I was no longer needed just because I was 65 years of age" (*Young or Old or In Between*).

He had been shoved into the category of "older persons."

Esther Pankratz also found aging disturbing. After forty-five years as a teacher of English she was lost and bewildered. She had enjoyed her students. "Young people are very wonderful," she says, "in what they can do to raise one's spirits." As the oldest in a family of ten, she had always been around people. A year before Esther's retirement, her mother, who had been living in Esther's home, died. This added to her sense of lostness.

Then a friend who owned a multiple housing unit in a nearby town offered her an apartment. She made the move, glad for a place that kept her in touch with people. After a time, a distant cousin working in the material aid center for their denomination's service organization invited her to work one day a week as a volunteer. Later, Esther was asked to give some time to a craft and thrift shop just being formed. Esther soon found her niche pricing the many books donated for sale. "I work when I want to and leave when I want to."

LOSING CONTROL AND FINDING HELP

Aging is a slow but steady process. After all, we began to age on the day we were born. But now in these later stages, aging moves on at a more rapid pace. At some point, many older adults have a sense of losing control. Once free and independent, they find themselves ever more dependent. They're not in charge of their own destiny. It doesn't feel good.

Where do older adults find help for the problems they face and the decisions they must make in the later years?

People of faith look to the faith community. Older adults need people who say, "We understand," who may also suggest, "Let's try this," who may even speak those good words, "You can do it."

We know the world will have to change. And the world will change if the church takes the lead in helping older adults face social and ethical issues unique to this period of life. What are these issues and how can the church guide in the process of decision making?

J. Winfield Fretz saw retirement coming. He had been a college administrator and teacher for forty years. He noted how leaders changed after they retired. "Their moods varied from bitterness, anger, self-depreciation, lack of self-confidence and even a total sense of futility," he said. He resolved early that would not happen to him.

These persons could not enjoy their new freedom. They missed their former status and prestige. "They were no longer considered or consulted about matters in which they formerly had the final word" (*Young or Old*). Now that Fretz himself has made the passage, he can look back. "We ought to define new and meaningful roles for the retired," he says. People who have been involved in making decisions for others still have work to do. "To stop making decisions is really demeaning."

He notes the large amount of time older persons have before them. "If society says retire at 65 and they live to be 90, that's 25 years, almost as long as an adult's productive work life before retirement." The community of faith can help older adults find ways to serve in the church and community. "Many congregations," says Leland Harder," are now giving more attention to a ministry of discerning the gifts of their members, putting to work the unused talents of their older adults" (*Young or Old*). But this requires that the congregation wrestle with its perception of older people and what they can do.

Henry A. Fast, whose story began this chapter, wrestled with retirement. He wanted to undertake it with dignity and without losing his sense of usefulness. Besides being a teacher, he had been active in Mennonite Central Committee, director of Civilian Public Service, and in touch with Mennonites in Europe and South America, as well as in the United States and Canada. He was a pioneer leader in the Mennonite mental health movement.

Fast received help from his church. It called him to be an administrator for the Board of Christian Service and later to be a member of the board. He had five good years as pastor of a church in Moundridge, Kansas. For one year, he was director of a senior voluntary service program for Mennonite Central Committee.

His gifts were widely recognized and established before he moved into this phase of his life. Laypersons, both men and women, need equal help in finding new roles for service through their congregation as they grow older.

Now eighty-nine, Esther Pankratz is not aware that her local congregation gave her special help in finding her way through her new stage in life. Yet the people who were there for her when she needed help were part of the larger serving network nurtured by the church.

HOW TO USE TIME AND MONEY WISELY

How do older adults use their time and money? One image of older adults is of persons who enjoy the good life after having worked hard and scrimped to save. Many now find pleasure in traveling and in recreation. "We're spending our children's inheritance," boasts the bumper sticker. Leisure activities and new experiences are the goal of some of them.

Some older adults are gone from home and home community half the year. They say they don't want to be tied down. "We've worked for it," they say to each other. "We deserve it."

"I'm beginning to wonder about that as a lifestyle," says Dorothea Janzen, associate pastor of Bethel College Mennonite Church, North Newton, Kansas, "especially when I think about all the jobs that need doing in the church."

Meanwhile, the work of the church and its mission of proclaiming the kingdom of God goes on. Does one contribute less financially during old age because income is less and health expenses are often greater?

"You have to wrestle with your conscience," says D.C. Wedel. "Do you still feel like sharing?" He sets aside one-tenth of his Social Security income for his local congregation. "And I want to hang on to my membership in the Bethel College President's Club [a donor club]," he says, "as long as I can."

Winfield and Marguerite Fretz have invested some funds in people. "In giving money to the poor," says Winfield, "we should be criticizing the system that keeps people poor." He notes that while people often talk of giving to the poor, they seldom talk about providing self-supporting opportunities for them.

"We're using our money to help people establish themselves in businesses and professions," he says. The Fretzes are providing capital not otherwise available to individuals through commercial channels. As older and experienced persons, they contribute counsel as well.

Older adults are frequently accused of contributing funds unwisely to organizations sponsored by televangelists. Some state they benefit from such programs and therefore would like to give something in return.

What is the task of the church in helping to donate money responsibly? Or is this always an individual decision?

In many places of the world, older adults are contributing to society by stepping in to help rear and care for grandchildren in the absence of parents due to domestic upheaval or work schedules. In the United States, 18 percent of all preschool children are being raised by grandparents, says Elbert C. Cole, founder of Shepherd's Centers of America.

People often feel that the basic needs of older persons are well cared for. They have access to subsidized housing, senior citizen centers, reduced fares on public transportation, visiting-nurse services, Meals on Wheels, and various commercial discounts. Those who benefit from these resources are more often the self-sufficient older adults than those who are poor, alone, and in ill health. What responsibility does the church have to correct this injustice? At what point in life need one no longer think of the needs of others?

Older single women are more likely to suffer from neglect and abuse than older men. The average older single woman lives alone on a low income in poor housing. She has poor medical care and has little chance to find a job, though a million older women must work to make ends meet. Employers are slow to hire older women because they see them as cantankerous, unattractive, emotional, and unreliable, though studies show that they make good employees. Women's rights groups have given little attention to the plight of the older woman. What can church groups or concerned Christians do to help this group?

WHERE TO FIND SUPPORT IN THE PURSUIT OF WELLNESS

Some older adults enjoy good health. Others do not. Who will care for me when I am old and sick? is a question many older people ask, especially single women without families. Is this an ethical issue? Parents who were once the caregivers for their children may need to depend on their children for care when they are older. Over all this looms the specter of needing long-term care in a nursing home. With such care now running between $25,000 and $30,000 a year, a stay of several years could quickly deplete the savings of many families.

Before making application for the nursing home, let's hear a word for wellness. Good health doesn't happen. Older adults have to work to get it and keep it even if they don't feel like it. That includes diet, exercise, eliminating smoking and drinking, and developing peace of mind. "The pursuit of wellness, even in retirement, is not a denial of the aging process nor of the reality of human death," says Erland Waltner, Elkhart, Indiana. Our faith as Christians, he says, is in a movement toward light and not into darkness. Good stewardship of our body means staying as healthy as possible so that the final illness will be as short as possible and not incur unnecessary expense.

"Seeking and finding wellness may be different for each person," says Waltner, "yet in congregations we can be supportive and helpful to one another in this quest." He notes that the Bible has "a great deal more to say about wholeness and health, including physical well-being, than I had ever observed before. The pursuit of wellness has become for me a part of Christian discipleship" (*Young or Old*).

In her congregation, Dorothea Janzen has charge of the pastoral care of the elderly, giving special attention to the twenty-seven members over ninety. "We have been individualistic," she says. "We need to help each other more."

She is looking at a plan for a nurse in the congregation to work on matters of wellness. Such a person or team would help members deal with the hard decisions relating to well-being. "It would be a work of the congregation," says Janzen.

Such a medical person or team might help older adults with wellness planning that would start with diet and exercise, and possibly start a group exercise program.

WHEN TO CONSIDER A NURSING HOME AND LONG-TERM CARE ALTERNATIVES

One of life's most difficult decisions is that of children who must place an elderly parent in a care facility against the parent's will. To many people the nursing home has become the place where the aged go to die a lingering death. And this, they believe will be the fate for most of the elderly. In fact, only two percent of the entire population, or about 4.6 percent of the elderly, will ever find themselves in a nursing home for a long term.

Most people live out their lives in their own homes. One out of five will be in an institution for certain periods. The nursing home is one place for those who need long-term care, but most communities now have a wider range of options. Some congregations have developed day-care centers for older adults. Home health care, day care, day hospitals, family support systems, and respite care may even prevent or delay the need for a nursing home. With the older population of many congregations increasing rapidly, should the church become as aggressively involved in developing alternatives to nursing homes as it once was in developing nursing homes and retirement centers?

Yet some few may need this kind of long-term care and are forced to confront it. Art DeHoogh, vice president of Newton (Kansas) Medical Center, works with families on financial and gift planning. "Responsible gift planners," he says, "suggest that assets be retained to provide for final expenses, such as long-term care. So, $100,000 is an amount that is reasonable to consider for this type of care."

Such a reserve may well be beyond the reach of many individuals or families. Even when possible, some may find that it does not pass the test of good stewardship. DeHoogh suggests other alternatives for the older person to consider, such as health insurance with a high deductible to cover catastrophic illness. Some life insurance policies now allow payouts for beneficiaries who are terminally ill and in nursing homes and whose status will not change.

HOW TO PLAN FOR THE FUNERAL AND FOR DEATH

Older persons find themselves attending funerals more often (or avoiding them more). Friends and kin are dying. Funerals witness to kingdom values. The grieving community becomes the supporting community. Faith in the living Christ is the hope of the older adult believer.

Congregations can help their members work through their concerns and ideas about death by encouraging groups to study issues of death and dying as well as funeral and burial practices. Should cremation be considered in large cities where burial plots are expensive and sometimes unavailable? Why has the church traditionally opposed cremation? Is burial in the ground a Christian tradition or one based on biblical principles?

What about the expense of funerals as a stewardship issue? Some congregations have purchased a funeral pall to lay over every coffin so that it makes no difference whether it is a highly expensive bronze casket or a lowly fabric-covered one.

A congregational study of death and funeral issues will include an emphasis on making a will for one's property and savings. Let there also be a living will to leave instructions on the use of life-sustaining procedures when one is approaching death. Copies of such intentions should be filed with physician, hospital, family, and church. Consider preparing a durable power of attorney for health care decisions. These steps can assure one's right to die with dignity.

Adults applying for membership in one congregation are asked to submit a plan for their funeral services. These plans are filed with those prepared by other members of the church, giving the pastoral staff and families a base for planning a service when a member dies. The act of writing out funeral instructions is an act of faith and a way of coping with the fact of death.

"One of the greatest gifts given to many older persons," says Harder, "is the serenity and trust with which they have prepared themselves for the coming death of their physical bodies, not with the morbid attitude of the fatalist, but in the spirit of the aging Paul, who wrote, "For to me, living is Christ, and dying is gain" (Phil. 1:21 NRSV).

THE CHURCH FAMILY REINVENTED

This new graying world in which we now live needs a special kind of church. We need a church in tune with the needs of people living longer with energy to work and serve Christ. Let it be a church that understands the needs of older adults. But be sure it is a church made up not of just one generation, but of three, four, even five generations. It will be a church reinvented for the living of these days.

In *Age Wave*, Ken Dychtwald and Joe Flower have written of the challenges and opportunities of an aging America. They see a different kind of world on the horizon, a world that needs a family reinvented. "As America ages," they say, "not only will we relate most closely with those blood and marital relatives with whom we feel the greatest affinity, but we will find in our networks of close friends, workmates, and neighbors the love, support, and companionship that our relatives cannot provide."

This family reinvented will be a "dramatic evolution in the structure and purpose of the American family." It will no longer be the nuclear, child-centered family. It will be bound together more by friendship and choice than by blood. Its lifeline will still be "love, caregiving, friendship and support" (Dychtwald).

Add to this description of the family a group of people knowing itself as the body of Christ, and we have a definition of the community of faith.

"If the church is truly a community, a place where sharing and caring take place," says Renee Sauder, a minister to women in ministry in the Mennonite Church, "then the world of the elderly need not be a lonely place" (*Young or Old*). Such a church will be the place to deal with life for young and old and those in between. Living and dying are always on the agenda of the faith community. Wellness, both physical, emotional and spiritual, is a concern.

Living and dying are special concerns for older adults in the congregation. But they are also concerns of youth and middle-aged adults. The words each age-group uses to speak of these concerns may sometimes differ, but at their core, they are the same. Thus the congregation, as the arena of dealing with life and death, has strength because it is intergenerational.

"Young people today need to hear and know that the welfare of older persons," says Paul Unruh, Prairie View Mental Health Center, "is dependent on opportunities given them to share with the younger generation what they have learned from life" (*Young or Old*). It is just as urgent for the older adult to hear from youth.

If we reinvent the church, what will be the configuration of retirement centers then? Will they include families with children? What about those communities with warmer climes to which older adults flock in winter? Will older adults find the support and nurture and opportunity for service in their home congregations if they choose not to go away?

Concerns for living and dying are not age-related questions. Caring for the aging, says Henri J.M. Nouwen, is not a special type of care. "When we allow our world to be divided into young, middle-aged, and old people, each calling for a specialized approach," he says, "then we are taking the real care out of caring, since the development and growth of men and women take place, first of all, by creative interaction among the generations" (*Aging: The Fulfillment of Life*). Older persons have a responsibility for the younger generation. Young people have a responsibility for older persons.

Answers to questions related to keeping meaning in life, lifestyle, wellness, investments, chronic illness, funerals, and many other issues do not come easily. They are answered for us in our living with other people in the caring faith community, not through retreat.

"If you have gathered nothing in your youth, how can you find anything in your old age?" (Sirach 25:3). Fortunate are those who have found love, peace, forgiveness, gentleness, kindness, and deep joy in their early years. They will have them as treasures to the end of their days. Let us dare to reinvent the church to be that kind of place for young and old.

TO THINK AND TALK ABOUT

1. Should one give up one's right to retire if one has a choice?

2. What principles should older people follow to establish a lifestyle that fits their Christian commitment? Will it be any different than for a younger person?

3. What is good use of time, energy, money, and influence as one grows older?

4. Are senior discounts a putdown? a marketing tool? an advantage earned by virtue of advanced age? a sign of respect for the older person? the reason prices are higher for younger folks?

5. What do frequent extended absences from family, church, and community to spend winters in warmer climes

do to relationships? Does the absence of many older people for significant periods of time deprive the church of their gifts and presence? Would they stay if they had a greater role in the church?

6. What factors should an older person and family consider before moving to a nursing home?

7. What is the responsibility of children to aging parents, including financial responsibility? What is the responsibility of aging parents to children? Who should be responsible for the care of older handicapped children? Who should look after whom?

8. How should the church respond to accusations of elder abuse in all forms, not only physical and verbal, but also economic, such as children helping themselves to parents' money or not providing clothing for parents in institutions?

9. How does the practice of funerals reveal our faith? In this age, when burial space is limited, is cremation acceptable for the believer?

10. How would you go about "reinventing" the church family?

What happens at death? What do the Old and New Testaments say about death? What do we mean by eternal life? by resurrection of the spirit and body? How can we deal with our own mortality and prepare for death? What gives us hope when a loved one dies?

Nigel M. de S. Cameron of Trinity Evangelical Divinity School writes that the world has almost squeezed out our Christian hope and condemned us to the values and fears of those who have no hope. "We have to keep learning the hopes and fears of the world to come," he writes. "That is what Christian living is all about, and if it doesn't make a difference when we stand face to face with death and dying, when will it?" (Christianity Today, April 6, 1992). Richard Gerbrandt offers some light on these issues.

CHAPTER 9

TOWARD DEATH: THE JOURNEY WE ALL TRAVEL

Richard Gerbrandt

Sooner or later every one of us will die. All human experience confirms the solemn words of divine revelation that "it is appointed for mortals to die once, and after that the judgment (Heb. 9:27, NRSV). For many persons the thought of death is frightening or even painful to think about. We want to see our grandchildren grow up. We want to travel. We want to enjoy our later years with our spouse. We feel we will miss out on much in life if we die. And yet, particularly as we reach fifty, sixty, and older, death becomes more and more a part of our daily lives. It takes our friends, our relatives, our mate, even our children.

Suddenly we reach an age at which we can no longer ignore death. We attend more funerals, and the reality of our own death is on our minds. We may not talk about it, but deep inside we are painfully aware that we, too, will face death and dying. The only way to escape death is never to have been born.

As human beings, we cannot ignore our mortality. But most of us wait until "later" to consider the inevitability of death. Few of us are prepared to die. In fact, our culture trains us to prepare for almost everything but death. Because death is certain and unavoidable, we need to deal in a straightforward manner with our mortality. As someone has said, "The mark of maturity is coming to grips with death." The intent of this chapter is to encourage us to be open about an experience we all face. Only during our lifetime can we prepare for death.

DENIAL, OUR AUTOMATIC TENDENCY

The denial of mortality suggests an instinctive fear of dying. If an individual becomes terminally ill, he or she can't count on being told the truth by family or physicians because they don't want to upset the patient. Some persons refuse medical analysis or treatment until it's too late. They're afraid they might hear bad news. People typically avoid or fear the subject of death. Older people are no exception. The reasons are varied.

1. *We may fear the process of dying.* Comedian Woody Allen affirms this fear when he quips, "I'm not afraid to die, but I'd rather not be there when it happens." I talked to a woman who for years had cared for her aging father. After he died, I asked her, "How are you handling your father's death?" Her reply: "It wasn't death that troubled me as much as the process of dying and the suffering he went through." We dread the journey to death, not the destination. Death itself may be welcome because it brings an end to suffering, pain, lengthy institutional care, or loss of dignity.

While I served as an associate pastor with Louis Paul Lehman, in Bakersfield, California, I often heard him say, "I pray that the Lord will take me home to be with him while I'm preaching the gospel." Graciously, God answered his prayer. He died participating in a Christmas Eve service.

Other people face extended periods of suffering. Miriam Armerding, wife of Hudson T. Armerding, president of Wheaton College (1965-82), was asked, "How do you handle this fear of debilitating illness?" Her answer: "Not easily. . . . I've prayed almost every day for the last five or six years, 'If it's your will, Lord, when you're finished with me, please take me quickly.' It's not my choice when to die. I can ask this of him, but it may not be his will. So I try to be sure that I'm completely committed to my Lord in this area—even if he should want me to be ill and incapacitated for the last year or months or days of my life."

2. *We fear the implications of separation from loved ones.* We don't want to let go of those we love. Each of us wants to see our children mature and to meet and hold our grandchildren. We want to finish our lives at a good old age. But the story is often otherwise: A newlywed husband or wife, who looks forward with joyous anticipation to a long life of marriage, is suddenly left with shattered dreams. A father dies, leaving his wife to raise their children alone. The elderly partner, who just celebrated fifty years of marriage, must face those final years alone.

3. *We fear giving up our strong attachments to the present life.*We have a business to run, places to go, agendas and projects to complete, events to attend—births, graduations, weddings of children and grandchildren. We have many valid and understandable reasons for not wanting to die, at least not yet. Our entrenchments bind us tightly to this life. To leave behind what we value and hold dear is painful.

4. *We fear the unknown future.* Who wants to step into a dark unknown? The fear of death can become a bondage similar to slavery says the writer of Hebrews (2:14-15).

This fear may come from failure to comprehend the truth of God's revelation regarding life after death. Paul reminds us that we can know "what God has prepared for those who love him" . . . because "God has revealed it to us by his Spirit" (1 Cor. 2:9b-10).

AN ISSUE SELDOM DISCUSSED

Whatever the reason for avoiding the topic of death, most of us find it hard to deal honestly and openly with it.

In the foreword to Elisabeth Kübler-Ross' book, *The Final Stage of Growth*, Joseph and Laurie Braga say that death is a subject that is "evaded, ignored, and denied by our youth-worshiping, progress-oriented society." They continue: "It is almost as if we have taken on death as just another disease to be conquered. But the fact is that death is inevitable. We will all die; it is only a matter of time." They point out that "death is not an enemy to be conquered or a prison to be escaped." They describe it as "an integral part of our lives that gives meaning to human existence." The prospect of death urges us to do something productive with whatever time is left to us.

While writers like Kübler-Ross have pushed us to deal with the reality and inevitability of death, it still remains a seldom-discussed issue, even among Christians who claim hope beyond the grave. There was a day when dying and death were more closely linked to living. Our great-grand-parents often died at home, surrounded by family and friends. Today death has become an institutional matter. Modern medical care, while sometimes giving the best treatment available, separates life from the dying process. People die in hospitals, often among strangers. The funeral industry "takes care of everything" and families are heard to say: "Let's get it over with quickly. We don't want a long service!"

David Dempsey in *The Way We Die* says: "Our society has secularized life. In so doing it has removed death from its traditional religious context, the belief that it is part of the natural order of things." If we can, even to a small degree, increase our understanding and acceptance of death, will we not face all of life with greater meaning and less fear?

The apostle James reminds us that human beings are "a mist that appears for a little while and then vanishes" (James 4:14, NIV). What then? What gives us hope when a loved one dies? Where do we find help to resolve fears and ques-tions that surround death? Experience simply vali-dates the fact that we will all die. Human reason offers little to console the breaking heart. Logic does not give peace and comfort. The Bible, however, gives us insight into death and immortality. In fact, all that can be known about life after death is a revelation from God.

THE MEANING OF DEATH

In the Bible death never denotes nonexistence. If human beings are made in the image of the eternal God, could they ever cease to exist?

The Christian hope of eternal life, as revealed in Scripture, is threaded through with three meanings of death:

1. *Physical death*, which is the separation of the soul (the spiritual part of humankind) from the body (the material part). While physical death is represented in Scripture as part of the penalty of sin, it ceases to be that for the Christian, since Christ has endured death as the penalty of sin for us. For the believer, death becomes a gateway through which the believer enters into the presence of the Lord.

2. *Spiritual death* is the separation of the soul (self) from God. This separation is the penalty of a fallen race, of which we are all a part. Because of sin, we are all separated from the presence and favor of God and need to be "made alive" from our spiritual deadness. The gospel of Jesus Christ is God's answer to spiritual death.

3. *Eternal death* is the completion of spiritual death. It is the eternal separation of the soul from God and the ultimate fate of unbelief. The apostle John calls it the "second death" (Rev. 2:11; 20:14; 21:8).

Whatever the reason we may have to deny death or fight off the inevitable, a believer has hope. That hope is founded in the Christian faith as presented in Holy Scripture. As we allow the Word of God to renew our thinking about death, we can move toward maturity and hope.

DEATH IN THE OLD AND NEW TESTAMENTS

Some Old Testament passages suggest that there is life after death but do not offer explicit details. Enoch (Gen.

5:24) and Elijah (2 Kings 2:11-12) were ushered into God's presence without dying. These events imply an immediate translation into the presence of God when their time on earth was complete. The prophet Balaam told Balak, King of Moab, after refusing to curse those whom God had not cursed: "Let me die the death of the righteous, and may my end be like theirs" (Num. 23:10, NIV). His words imply hope and life with God when the journey on earth is over.

Job, in his difficult trials, asked the question, "If a man dies, will he live again?" He answers his own question with compelling words reaching for the great truth: "I know that my Redeemer lives." He assures himself that after his body has been destroyed, he will see God in his flesh. "I myself will see him with my own eyes—I, and not another" (Job 19:25-27). While the meaning of this passage is not absolutely clear, he asserts his hope that a Redeemer will finally vindicate his good name. Since there are no human volunteers, God is his only hope.

The prophets, especially in the apocalyptic books, give us some of the strongest Old Testament statements concerning resurrection after death. The prophet Isaiah proclaims boldly, "But your dead will live; their bodies will rise. . . . the earth will give birth to her dead" (Isa. 26:19, NIV).

The prophet Daniel speaks of a time when those "whose names are found written in the book will be delivered" (Dan. 12:1-2). Multitudes of people who "sleep in the dust of the earth will awake." Some will awake to everlasting life and others to everlasting death.

The prophet Hosea writes, "I will ransom them from the power of the grave; I will redeem them from death. Where, O death, are your plagues? Where, O grave, is your destruction?" (13:14, NIV).

Each of these passages, while not a clear, direct promise of life after death, in the words of Daniel J. Simundsen, contains the seed of hope that death does not end all.

The New Testament declares more explicitly the assurance that death does not have the final word. While death does have its sorrow and pain, the believer does not "sorrow as those who have no hope" (1 Thess. 4:13). The New Testament writers offer Christians a hope that is sure, a comfort in sorrow, yes, encouragement in the face of death that "we will be with the Lord forever."

At the grave of Lazarus, Jesus spoke to Martha, his sorrowing sister, words of promise regarding life after death: "I am the resurrection and the life. He who believes in me will live, even though he dies; and whoever lives and believes in me will never die" (John. 11:23-26). He also speaks words of comfort and hope to his disciples, assuring them that he is not deserting them but rather preceding them into glory to prepare a place for them. And if he goes and prepares a place for them, he will come back and take them to be with him where he is (John 14:1-3).

Do we believe these words? Can we trust the words of Holy Scripture? Faith in Christ freed Paul from fear of death should he journey to Jerusalem. He stated boldly he was ready to be taken prisoner, but also "to die in Jerusalem for the name of the Lord Jesus" (Acts 21:13).

The ancient philosopher Plato once said: "The hour of departure has arrived and we go our ways. I to die, and you to live. Which is better God only knows." But we know something of which Plato was unaware. We, with Paul, have come to understand that "to die is gain," and that "to depart and be with Christ" is better by far (Phil. 1:20-23). Paul writes: "If we live, we live to the Lord; and if we die, we die to the Lord. So, whether we live or die, we belong to the Lord" (Rom. 14:8, NIV). For those of us who belong to the Lord, death is simply an extension of life and not to be feared. Death is the means of gaining the inheritance of a prepared place where God dwells. Paul encourages the Corinthians with hope in the resurrection of Christ. If the resurrection of Jesus was not a fact, then the whole Christian message was based on a lie, and those who died believing it had trusted in an untruth (1 Cor. 15:12-19). The resurrection of Christ is the foundation of the gospel.

First Corinthians 15 contains that great resurrection message and rises to a victorious climax with the saying taken from the words of the prophet Isaiah (25:8), "Death has been swallowed up in victory" (1 Cor. 15:54) and from the prophet Hosea, "Where, O death, are your plagues? Where, O death is your destruction?" (13:14, NIV). Paul, who, one day on that Damascus road, had turned from spiritual death to new life in Christ, concludes the chapter with his victory prayer, "But thanks be to God! He gives us the victory through our Lord Jesus Christ" (1 Cor. 15:57, NIV).

The resurrection of Jesus Christ is the climactic truth of the New Testament that moves us from the fear of death to a vibrant hope (1 Pet. 1:3-4). While the physical body "sleeps" for a while, it will be changed, "in a flash, in the twinkling of an eye, at the last trumpet." Paul states that the dead will be raised "imperishable," and every believer will be changed (1 Cor. 15:52-53). That is to say that in God's chosen hour, when Christ comes again, our souls, separated from the body at the time of death, will be reunited with a new resurrected body like Christ's resurrection body. That is our hope as children of God. Simundson writes, "As Christians, the resurrection of Jesus is still the strongest symbol we have to remind us that our hope is not illusory, not mere wishful thinking, but based solidly on the defeat of death, once and for all, by God's own Son" (*Hope for All Seasons*).

Following the final judgment, this hope is translated into the reality of a new heaven and a new earth in which God dwells with his people. The apostle John describes this new state: "I saw the Holy City, the New Jerusalem, coming down out of heaven from God, prepared as a bride beautifully dressed for her husband." In this new earth God "will wipe every tear from their eyes. There will be no more death or mourning or crying or pain, for the old order of things has passed away" (Rev. 21:1-4, NIV).

WHAT HAPPENS AT THE TIME OF DEATH?

We have reviewed key Scripture references regarding death. However, questions still remain regarding our state following death. Do believers enter into the presence of God immediately? Only a few Bible passages deal with this important question. But clearly the Bible teaches that believers will immediately be translated into the presence of God. Enoch and Elijah, while exceptions to physical death, were both translated into the presence of God when their time on earth was over.

Jesus told the penitent thief on the cross that he would be with him in paradise on the very day he died (Luke 23:43). Paradise represents, to the best of our understanding, the locality where the souls of the righteous find residence after death. Some writers equate paradise with "Abraham's bosom" from the account of the rich man and Lazarus in Luke 16. When Lazarus died, the angels carried him to Abraham's side. Both consciously recognized each other, and, in fact, conversed together. As Stephen was being stoned he looked up and said, "Lord Jesus, receive my spirit" (Acts 7:59).

The apostle Paul states that when we depart this life, that is, when the soul separates from the body, the believer is with the Lord. He writes to the Philippian believers: "I desire to depart and be with the Lord" (1:23). In his letter to the Corinthian church he contrasts being "at home in the body and away from the Lord" with being "away from the body and at home with the Lord" (2 Cor. 5:6-8). In both references he speaks of being "with the Lord." The passages that speak of death as "sleep" refer to the sleep of our bodies in the place of the dead, awaiting the day of resurrection, while our souls are with the Lord.

The Scriptures present the believer's passage to heaven as a direct route into the presence of our Lord, an event that happens at death. Billy Graham says in *Facing Death,* "The moment we take our last breath on earth, we take our first in heaven." In God's time, at the coming of Christ, our souls will be given glorified and resurrected bodies. "And so we will be with the Lord forever" (1 Thess. 4:17, NIV).

HOW THEN SHOULD WE FACE DEATH?

1. *By receiving God's gift of eternal life through Jesus Christ.* Read again what Christ does for those who are "dead in transgressions and sins." The security of knowing we are

spiritually alive because of our relationship to Jesus Christ removes much of the "sting" of death.

2. *By recognizing that death is a transition.* The transition for the unbeliever into the next life is different than for the Christian. Sadly, death for the unbeliever is punitive, the penalty for sin, and does not come merely as a result of natural law. Paul speaks of the "sting of death" for those still in their sin (1 Cor. 15:56). The transition for those outside of Christ is to an eternal separation from God and results in eternal punishment (Rev. 20:12-15).

However, God is full of mercy and abounding in love. No one needs to face the sting of death. The gospel is clear that "whoever believes in him shall not perish but have eternal life" (John 3:16). Believers, those who have placed their faith in Jesus Christ, see death as a transition from the physical body into the presence of the Lord.

The apostle Paul also speaks of death as a departure. "The time has come for my departure," he writes young Timothy (2 Tim. 4:6). Lehman Strauss points out in *When Loved Ones Are Taken in Death* that the word *departure* is used metaphorically as when a ship pulls up anchor and sets sail, or as when an army breaks camp to move on. In the ancient Greek world this term was used also to describe the act of freeing someone from chains. As Strauss says, "Here we are anchored to the hardships and heartaches of this life. In death the gangway is raised, the anchor is weighed and we set sail for the Golden Shore. In death we break camp here to start for heaven."

3. *By restructuring our attitudes toward death.* While believers do sorrow in the face of death, we do so with a different attitude. We do not deny or conceal our pain. Rather, we sorrow with hope. John, after hearing a voice from heaven, wrote "Blessed are the dead who die in the Lord" (Rev. 14:13, NIV). Paul speaks of his desire to depart and be with Christ, which is far better. He also says that to "die is gain." Gain? Isn't death a loss? No, it is gain in the face of loss. As Christians, we need to bring our thinking with regard to death in line with the Word of God so that we see it as a

step forward, not backward. How we handle the subject of death is dependent, in part, on how we think about this inevitable step in the life process.

4. *By rejoicing in the hope of the resurrection of Jesus Christ from the dead.* What we call death is not the end. Jesus clearly told the disciples that even though people die physically, those who believe in him will see life. In this sense, we never die (John 11:25-26). This hope is linked directly and foundationally to Christ's resurrection. Jesus promises, "Because I live, you also will live" (John 14:19). When we come to grips with the meaning and impact of Christ's resurrection we can begin to see dying as triumph. "Death has been swallowed up in victory" (1 Cor. 15:54, NIV).

5. *By relinquishing ownership of the things that bind us to this life.* As human beings we own nothing. We are but stewards of what God has entrusted to our care. The belief that we own anything is pagan. The Scriptures instruct us to shift from holding on to what we think we own to making a deposit in the life to come.

We are well aware that our good works go on before us. It is harder to recognize that our material possessions can be sent on ahead also. Is that not what Jesus was telling his listeners when he said, "Where your treasure is, there your heart will be also" (Matt. 6:19-21). Exchanging earthly values for heavenly values through faithful, sacrificial stewardship underscores our longing for heaven and lessens our ties to this life. Planning our estate to include the continuance of God's work are ways of "laying up treasures in heaven."

6. *By realizing that our citizenship is in heaven.* The writer of Hebrews encourages us from the faith and life of Abraham, who was looking forward to "the city with foundations, whose architect and builder is God" (Heb. 11:10). Abraham, along with other heroes of faith "admitted that they were aliens and strangers on earth." Peter carries on this same theme, challenging the scattered believers to live their lives "as strangers here in reverent fear . . . as aliens and strangers in the world" (1 Pet. 1:17; 2:11, NIV). Let's live out the words of that song, "This world is not my home,

I'm just a-passin' through."

7. *By readying ourselves for the inevitability of death.* The prophet reminded King Hezekiah to put his house in order, "because you will die." Dr. Charles Hodge once said, "It is important that when we come to die we have nothing to do but to die." It is wise to prepare to die before the reality of death is forced on us.

The certainty of death confronts us with additional tasks:

* *To bring our lives into harmony with the will of God* (James 4:14-15). An obedient life most surely clears the agenda for facing death and meeting God. A life lived in harmony with the will of God frees us from much of the fear associated with dying.

* *To restore broken relationships while we can.* Too many believers suffer emotional pain throughout much of life because of unresolved conflict, particularly between parents and children, but also between spouses, family members, and with former teachers and pastors. Dealing with such issues while time allows pays a double benefit. One, we open the door to healing for those we leave behind. Two, we prepare ourselves to face death free from the anguish of ending life with an unfinished agenda.

* *To prepare our estate while we have clear minds.* Estate planning includes thinking through how to lay up treasures in heaven. It includes determining our heirs. Should we leave it all to the children? Andrew Carnegie once said, "No [one] has the right to handicap [a child] with such a burden as great wealth." Including the church as an heir in our will ensures that the work of the kingdom of God will continue.

* *To make it as easy as possible for loved ones to deal with our final days.* Advance directives through a living will and durable power of attorney ensure our wishes will be respected when death comes. A portfolio of the location of important documents and instructions regarding funeral arrangements help our confused and brokenhearted loved ones.

* *To leave some written memories.* When we leave behind a written, voice, or video record of our life story we express love and hope for children and grandchildren. Ruth died a

few weeks ago. Recognizing the frailty of her physical condition, she took time to write her memories about each child and grandchild before she died. She recounted the special experiences she had had with each person, leaving behind a beautiful gift of love.

* *To talk about death.* We need not make death a morbid preoccupation, but we can bring it out of the closet and converse with family and friends on the subject. Bible study and open discussion of the subject of death clarifies misconceptions and helps us adjust our attitudes. The one reality in life we will all experience should not be given the silent treatment. The essence of the Christian life is to live this life for God and to prepare for our journey to God's eternal heaven. It's important enough to talk about.

"For the believer, death is not the end but the beginning. Faith sees beyond death and grasps God's promise of eternal life," writes I. Langstan Haygood. "Death is necessary. It is a door to heaven." (*Discipleship Journal*, 62:1991). Let us then take a new and fresh look at both our frail mortality and our hope of immortality. This hope may have become vague, if not lost in the attachments that bind us to this life. Let us, like Abraham, declare that we are but "aliens and strangers on earth." When we detach ourselves from what is temporary in this life, we can accept that death is not the end but rather the beginning of life in another country, a better country—a heavenly one, whose architect and builder is God (Heb. 11). God has planned something better for the believer (Heb. 11:40).

TO THINK AND TALK ABOUT

1. What reservations or fears do you have that may cause you to deny or ignore the subject of death?

2. What shifts in your feelings and thinking do you need to make to bring them in line with what Scripture says about death?

3. What is the best way to respond to an elderly person who wishes to die but who is not in immediate danger of

dying? or to one who has given up on life? What brings meaning and hope?

4. How can the topic of death be reintroduced into the family and the faith community setting? If members of your group are familiar with the hospice movement, have them describe what happens.

Intimate relationships make a profound difference in the quality of life at any age. Yet, in the later years, the making and keeping of relationships can be difficult. Sometimes there are fewer of them because of physical limitations and living arrangements. How does growing older became an opportunity to learn new patterns of intimacy and communication? The church needs to be intentional in embracing older persons, writes James H. Waltner. "The church will either be an integrating force in the life of the older person or it will be a disintegrating force."

CHAPTER 10

WHO WILL BE WITH ME WHEN I AM OLD?

James H. Waltner

My childhood memories include Grandpa and Grandma. They lived with us. My father, the youngest son in the family, took over the home farm when he married. With that privilege came also the responsibility of providing a home for his parents until their death.

Grandpa died at age 83 when I was ten, and Grandma the next year. I remember that Grandpa traveled, usually to Canada, to visit friends. He told fascinating stories when he returned. Grandma darned socks, shelled peas, baked bread, and let us go to sleep on the couch in her room when our parents went away for the evening. Many times I heard her say evening prayers. On Sunday we often had visitors—uncles and aunts, cousins, and others from the neighborhood and church who came to see Grandpa and Grandma. As a young boy I sensed that my grandparents enjoyed their many friendships with relatives, neighbors, and church community.

"Intimate relationships make a profound difference in the quality of life at any age," say Ken Dychtwald and Joe Flower, authors of *Age Wave*. Yet in the later years of life, making and keeping relationships can become more difficult. Erik Erikson states that one of the developmental tasks of the young adult is to learn intimacy, a task that continues throughout life. By intimacy he means the ability to love and commit oneself to particular persons, to share deeply with others.

Evelyn Eaton Whitehead and James D. Whitehead describe intimacy as an "overlapping of space, a willingness to be influenced, an openness to the possibility of change" (*Christian Life Patterns*). It comes into play in friendships, when working together, and in community living. They state that intimacy is not just communal. A person can become more intimate with oneself, open to what is happening in the inner being in the present but also to what happened in the past and dealing with it.

With aging, the roles and positions of family members change. The average family is now often composed of four generations. When children leave home, Mom and Dad must become Mary and John to one another again. Retirement for one or both spouses means more time spent together, sometimes causing tensions. Loss of spouse means a greater dependence on friends of the same gender and on children. Health problems sometimes cause withdrawal from extended family activities.

Grandparenting and great-grandparenting introduce new joys, but also concerns. Inability to look after one's own needs as an older person puts new responsibilities on adult children, who may at the same time be overburdened with the care of their own teenage or young adult children. New family roles may create competition for time and money.

How does growing older become an opportunity to learn new patterns of intimacy and communication? Who will be with me when I am old, asks the older person. What are the roles of spouse, family, friends, and the church in fostering intimacy and providing relationships that enhance life?

THE SPOUSE

"When our last child left home," writes columnist Erma Bombeck, "a friend called and said, 'You need company to get you through the first night alone?'"

"Actually," responded Erma, "you caught us as we were leaving. We're going out to dinner."

University of Nebraska researchers on the empty-nest syndrome discovered that when children leave home the marriage of the parents not only improves, but that the couple may even experience a mini-honeymoon.

For persons who share life in marriage, the older years can be rewarding years for the enjoyment of companionship and affection. George Santayana, Spanish American poet and philosopher, observed that "the spirit can enter a human body perhaps better in the quiet of old age and dwell there more undisturbed than in the turmoil of adventure." Less personal ambition and aggressiveness is part of the mellowing that allows spouses to respond to each other in ways that nurture.

Retirement from the heavier responsibility of earlier years often allows marriage partners more freedom for daily walks, hobbies, travel, conversation over tea, and simply "to be." For many, the relationship becomes more intimate again. There may be more time and desire and freedom for sexual expression of affection. Studies of sexual behavior indicate that many married persons continue to have active sexual relationships into their eighties and nineties, write Robert M. Gray and David O. Moberg in *The Church and the Older Person.* Holding hands, touching, hugging, sexual intimacies, are deepened by the life experiences the couple has shared and by a profound sense of God's grace through the years.

Spouses increasingly nurture each other and become caregivers to each other. A husband who stayed clear of the kitchen may become chief cook because of his wife's declining eyesight or because he has discovered the joy of cooking. A wife becomes the steadying arm and driver for a husband who cannot walk alone. The married, among the old, hold hands a lot, out of love and affection, and to steady one another. One older woman commented to her daughter that sometimes she and her elderly frail husband, when overwhelmed by the difficulties they faced in old age, simply stood in the living room and physically "clung to each other."

THE FAMILY

We need one another for wholeness. In the forest ecosystem, each plant and animal is essential; the loss of one species sets off a cycle of upheaval and disruption. The family is also an ecosystem; at every age family members play unique and essential roles, writes Tilman Smith in an unpublished article, "Needs and Desires of Older Persons Today."

Lena, though never married, was part of a family. A college professor for many years, she invested her life in her students. In addition to the campus community, her circle included neighbors, the church, and professional colleagues. But she also corresponded with and visited her brothers, nephews and nieces, and their children. Upon retirement from teaching, she remained in her home for a few years. Now the question loomed: "Who will be with me when I am old?"

Lena turned to her family. Recognizing that she would likely outlive neighbors and peers where she lived, she made the decision to move back to her home community where she had family. "At least there I'll have nephews and nieces who will stop to see me." And they did.

Whether married or single, adults do well to cultivate good relationships with children, their own and those of others. Young adult children often grow in their affection for their parents. They forgive and forget the tense situations that occurred during the time they wanted independence. Their love and respect for their parents increases when they become parents. Grandchildren provide a new bond for the generations. The joy of grandparenting includes seeing grandchildren become young adults and begin their families. The presence of the little ones in a family speaks hope to older persons.

Family members often are the first line of caregivers for older persons. The dilemma for increasing numbers of those caregivers is that they are older adults themselves. Dr. Joseph Francis, assistant professor of geriatrics at the University of Pittsburgh School of Medicine, says, "We have in our clinic 95-year-old patients who are being taken care of by 75-year-old daughters, who haul them out of bed, dress them and feed them. It's very, very difficult when the children are having their own set of medical problems." Older caregivers need an extra measure of support from their own children, friends, and church community to survive this stressful period.

Time was when the needs of the dependent elderly were primarily met by their children. However, the conditions of urban life, the decline in birth rates, and the longevity of many people is changing all that.

FRIENDS

The emotional pain of loneliness can affect humans of all age, but the elderly know it best. Single or widowed older adults are especially vulnerable to feelings of emptiness from losses that occur in later life. However, even a married person can suffer from loneliness. Loneliness is different from solitude or aloneness since loneliness often occurs in the presence of other individuals. It refers to the feeling of incompleteness at the loss of intimate relationships. Loneliness comes when we want to share our feelings with someone and there is no one there. Solitude is the state of being alone, but not feeling uncomfortable with that aloneness.

In reality 65 percent of elderly females live alone or with non-relatives. Most of them are widowed. They ask, not assertively, but in the silence of their hearts, sometimes to friends, "Who will be my friends? Who becomes a friend when my peers are dying?"

"If people want to be happy when they're old, they should store up happy memories when they are young," writes Alaric W. Blair in *The Elkhart Truth*. So two friends at the Greencroft Retirement Center in Goshen, Indiana, help each other enjoy life by recalling happy memories from many decades ago when they raised their families in south Texas.

When a stroke impaired her lifelong friend, Edna boarded her three-wheeled cart and rode over to the nursing center to visit Nona. "I remember being down ill and Edna would come over every day so faithfully to cheer me up," Nona said.

Later, Nona could return these kind gestures when Edna was ill. "I collect quotations and on those days that I cannot get over and visit, I send Edna a letter with one of the quotations. But when we do get together, we talk for hours" (Nona Kauffman and Edna Stoltzfus in *The Elkhart Truth*).

Earl, whose legs were both amputated because of a debilitating illness, entered a nursing home at the age of sixty-five. His wife came to see him regularly, as did other family members. Physically, Earl was increasingly confined to his room. How does one stay mentally and spiritually alive during years of such limited contact with people? How does one keep up interest in what is happening in community, church, and nation? More than one older person admits, "I have nothing to talk about anymore. Nothing happens in my life anymore." Weak eyesight prevents reading and television is unappealing.

Earl had four friends who visited him regularly. A college classmate had sung with him in a quartet on deputation trips. Another had been a medical student in the same community where Earl was a young pastor. Another had been his teacher in college. And a fourth, who came every Friday evening, brought the newspaper, his church periodical, and a Bible. These friends from an earlier period of their lives shared experiences. They became Earl's eyes and ears to the world through the tough days and years, companions sharing faith and hope until his "homegoing."

Many volunteer programs for older adults have developed to capitalize on the skills, energy, and time of older adults. Some find these contacts in other ways to build new friendships. But it takes imagination as well as determination to make new friends as old ones slip away.

THE CHURCH

A new business that developed in Japan recently has the name, "Rent-A-Family." In that society, family ties have traditionally been strong. Now 60 percent of older persons live apart from family; many live alone. For a fee, older persons can rent "children" and "grandchildren" for a meal, holiday, or ritual festival. "I just wanted someone to call me Dad," explained a lonely old man.

The church provides extended family experiences for many of its members, although some contend that congregations are couple-centered in their programming and emphases. The truth is that in some congregations up to 30 to 40 percent of the members are single or live alone—widows, widowers, separated or divorced, or persons who have never married. If the church is the church, it will be the extended family to a wide range of persons.

If the priesthood of all believers and the spirit of community have special meaning for us not only do older members have responsibility to instruct the next generation, but persons of all ages have gifts for the benefit of the whole body—and this includes older adults. Gray and Moberg write that the church can help correct the mistaken idea that "old age is an unimportant period of life when the individual can no longer be active and can no longer contribute."

Older members have skills, wisdom, and experience to share. In the church the Spirit helps to discern the special gifts and needs of the elderly, along with the related opportunities. What can older adults do in the church? They can engage in public and private prayer, teach, visit, improve and maintain church property, do clerical work, child care, work as community service volunteers, counsel, and help in countless other ways.

Modern work mobility often fragments the nuclear family, thus setting the stage for the church to act as the extended family for all ages. In intergenerational groups in the church, families can "adopt" grandparents, older persons can "adopt" a family or grandchildren. The benefits of such relationships are far-reaching. Most important, it gives older people a sense of being needed.

Paul Tournier, in *Learning to Grow Old*, suggests: "We must learn to love the old (as we have learned since Rousseau to love the young) for who they are—simply persons—not for what they can (or can't) do for us anymore."

The nature of the gospel requires that the church address its witness and mission to the needs, desires, and potential of older adults. The church does not remain neutral. It will either be an integrating force in the life of the older person or it will be a disintegrating force. We dare not see life's later passages or stages as denigrations. We must see older adults as having growth potential, writes Al Sloat, in *Journal of Adult Training* (Summer 1989), and recognize them as being valuable in their own right because of their maturity and wisdom.

We must communicate to older persons that the church loves and appreciates them and that they are an important part and ministry of the church. Psychologist Dorothy Gish of Messiah College provides ten commandments for behavior with and toward older adults.

1. Thou shalt maintain regular contact with them.
2. Thou shalt include them in celebrations.
3. Thou shalt be imaginative in gift giving.
4. Thou shalt listen thoughtfully to reminiscences.
5. Thou shalt not gloss over their worries and/or complaints.
6. Thou shalt not embarrass or distress them.
7. Thou shalt not undermine their self-respect or assurance.
8. Thou shalt be on their side.
9. Thou shalt be sympathetic toward them.
10. Thou shalt not forget to laugh with them.

("The Aging: Myths, Needs, Ministry," *The Asbury Seminarian*, 39:1984)

Among characteristics of older adults is their interest in relationships, including touch. Anyone who spends time with older adults understands the importance of hugs. Like children, older people sense a necessity for touching and feeling. There's security in strong, warm embraces—not just a clasped hand or an arm around the shoulder— but a literal and genuine "hands-on approach." Tactile relationships take on as great an importance in working with older adults as they do in childhood education, writes Kenneth Gangel in *Journal of Adult Training* (Summer 1989).

Older persons also need affirmation. They quickly catch the innuendoes in remarks such as, "You look pretty good for a person of your age." They want to be thought of as individuals, not as a member of a group. Their age makes people forget they are people with sensitivities just like any other person. Calling a person by name is important in any phase of education, but more important here because older persons have a tendency to feel they are viewed only as "old people," rather than as Jane, Tom, Jack, or Dorothy. Respect strengthens affirmation.

Another characteristic of older adults is their need for mental stimulation. They need "new and now" approaches. For some, there really is no tomorrow. Creativity and adventure, if they're going to be experienced, need to be experienced now. Young adults look to the future; middle adults concern themselves with security. But living in the present is absolutely crucial for older adults. They need to be encouraged to explore new ideas, new skills and given the psychological freedom and safety to do so. Their creative attitudes and powers often lie unused and rusty and need some kind of catalyst to get them started.

The church can help older persons let go of grudges and bitterness. Aging is a time for reconciliation. Carrying seeds of unforgiveness is a dead weight one can ill afford to carry. So the church can help keep open the lines of communication between people, their families, and friends. But older persons can also teach about the wisdom of forgiveness because they are persons who have been forgiven and have learned to forgive. This can be done by visiting with them, arranging for sharing times, and giving them freedom to tell their life pilgrimage in appropriate settings.

With increasing age the choices for intimacy narrow. Spouse, friends, and children die. The question persists: Who will be with me when I am old? Hopefully no older persons must make the end journey alone, but will find their lives in the keeping of God. So Roy Larson, former *Chicago Sun-Times* religion editor, wrote, "We may not be able to play sandlot football on Saturdays anymore, and we may experience the ravages of living in 'the age of never,' but we can . . . for sure, learn to live closer to the eternal 'center of surprise' whose proper name is God."

Commenting on the letter to the Corinthians, Larson adds, "There is a part of us that goes from dust to dust, from ashes to ashes. There is also a part of us, no less real, that goes from glory to glory. The promise is that we can grow in grace as we grow in years—if we keep open the channels to the soul . . . and prepare . . . to meet our God" (*Context*).

So the church needs to be intentional in strengthening the faith of older persons and also in embracing them as members of the community of faith. Intergenerational groups, adopt-a-family, adopt-a-grandparent, mentoring relationships, reading and relating to older persons who are homebound or in nursing homes, provide a richness all generations need. We will then find the lives of old and young empowered.

A final suggestion to answer the question, "Who will be with me when I am old?" has to do with the pastor's relationship to older persons. Who will be a pastor to me when I am old?

I hope the person will be a pastor who is not afraid of growing older or of the old.

I want that pastor to be someone who will do active listening, who will respond in ways that will encourage me to elaborate, to reminisce, and so to recapture previous inner strength and feelings of self-worth.

I want that pastor to be a person who represents God

and the community of faith to me.

I want that pastor to share hope and not be afraid to pray with me, to sit with me, to touch me, and to hang in there with me when I finally walk through the valley of the shadow of death.

Who will be with me when I am old? Zechariah paints this lovely portrait of the restored Jerusalem: "Old men and old women shall again sit in the streets of Jerusalem, each with staff in hand [because of their great age]. And the streets of the city shall be full of boys and girls playing in its streets" (Zech. 8:4-5, RSV).

TO THINK AND TALK ABOUT

1. Find out the number of adults in your congregation over the age of sixty-five. How many are married or single? How many live in nursing homes or retirement centers? How many are still mobile (i.e. able to drive a car)?

2. What assurance can you give older single persons without relatives nearby that they will not be alone in their later years?

3. What suggestions do you have for older adults who are not very mobile or outgoing on how to maintain intimacy in their lives?

4. Intimacy is often confused with sexual experience and romance, but it actually means making oneself vulnerable and available to another. What stories in the Bible can you think of that illustrate intimacy? Consider the story of Jacob wrestling with the angel, Jesus and the disciples at the Last Supper, and some of the conversations between Moses and God.

5. Older people often prefer letters to phone calls because it gives them something to return to again and again. Would you recommend installing fax machines in retirement centers?

6. Can you think of some older adults who exhibit a creative approach to life? What keeps that spark of creativity alive in them?

PART III

GRACE: QED

*T*homas a Kempis, *in* Imitation of Christ, *states that they "travel lightly whom God's grace carries." Some people observe the serene manner of some older people and wonder how they are able to maintain that quiet confidence and inner peace despite a long life burdened by life's tumults. That question can be answered with just two words:* God's grace.

Laban and Helen Peachey's teachers in grace probably can't explain how they achieved strength for living, though their bodies are fragile, or how they were able to shift from independent living to dependent living with confident peace of mind. Learning to draw on God's grace and maintain hope cannot be reduced to a set of techniques and explained in a how-to manual, although Paul M. Miller's interviewees offer some suggestions. We can never trace exactly where the work of God's Spirit began and the circuitous route it may have taken.

Grace is always a supernatural work of God. It is not founded in our human capacity to endure, but on trust in God's daily providence. The German language has a beautiful word for this attitude, Gelassenheit, *meaning deliberate composure, calmness and resignation, yet not becoming a milksop. For the Christian,* Gelassenheit *means a deliberate resignation to God's working in our lives. All we have and are is by God's overflowing favor.*

In high school, after we had successfully done a geometry problem, we wrote QED (quod erat demonstrandum) *at the end, meaning "which was to be proven or demonstrated." Task accomplished.*

Older people are the QED of life: Which was to be proven. God's grace did it all. The problem has been solved. They have been stamped with God's nature. To God be the glory.

Elbert C. Cole, speaker at one of the Inter-Mennonite Conferences on Aging in the spring of 1992, points out that "older adults need to stand in society and pass the word to each younger generation that they can 'make it.' Collectively, they can tell their stories and they can demonstrate the 'how' and the 'what,' and ask each younger generation to pass this support along." He points out that older adults can describe those times they learned to "sacrifice or sublimate" their own desires because they valued another person. They can tell younger people "there was pain and burden along the way" but they "stood steady when things shook and found strength." He concludes that older adults have the obligation and the privilege to recount the times in their lives when they, too, didn't think they could make it, but did—and that means the next generation can too!

Helen Wade Alderfer introduces storytelling from her unique viewpoint, as one who enjoys sharing her own story and encouraging others to tell theirs.

CHAPTER 11

YOU HAVE A STORY TO TELL

Helen Wade Alderfer

D o you know how one-of-a-kind you are? I can remember the day and the desk at which I sat in grade school, when I learned that there are no two fingerprints alike in the whole world. My world was small then, so I couldn't know how many people there were in the world; I only knew the number was many. Much later I was astonished by the knowledge that there are no two voices alike in the world.

And then, one day, the thought that every person has an unduplicated set of memories came home to me with sad clarity. My father-in-law's death brought me sorrow because he was a good father-in-law whose death was a loss to me, and because it came to me that all the experiences and memories of that man were now lost. Only as those who knew him recounted the stories of his life would he be remembered.

Fingerprints, voices, memories—all affirm that we are indeed "fearfully and wonderfully made" (Ps. 139:14a).

When someone says, "Oh, I don't have anything to tell about my life," it may be a sign of a lack of awareness of the person's uniqueness. Remember the story of the sparrow that does not fall to the ground without the Father's watchful eye? It means that your story and mine have value to us and others. That richness will be recognized when we give it a place.

WHY SHARE YOUR STORY?

People have been writing and telling their stories for a long time. I am often touched by the stories of the lives of persons long gone; the light of their candles still burns for us today through their writings. In primitive cultures, families and tribes gathered around firesides to hear their elders share the wisdom of the past in stories. In more modern times, families gather around dining room tables and on patios, at family reunions and church services, at quiltings and coffee breaks, to talk about another time, another place. Immigrants often bring to this land only memories and values—that is all they have to pass on.

Sharing one's story has many benefits:

Continuity with the past. Sharing your story establishes continuity with the past. You didn't come to the present moment without a past. That past, when given a place, can add meaning to the present.

Your story is an incomparable gift for another—for children, grandchildren, nieces and nephews. It forges a link in the chain of family life. When Alice Harrison at age seventy decided to write her life story, she said, "I am writing for my great-grandchildren to whom it is wholly dedicated." How I wish my maternal grandmother had kept a journal on the long ocean voyage from Europe to America in 1885. With husband, eight children (small Joseph was buried in

Switzerland), was it a time of great fears? Were there unexpected joys, too? Did faith help the journey?

William Fletcher writes in *Recording Your Family History* that storytelling represents "an intuitive response to a deeply felt need for a sense of personal and family continuity" in a quickly changing world. He points out that millions of people yearn "to reconnect in some way with the continuity of their family's experience," a continuity once taken for granted.

Sharing your faith. More than a genealogical account, your story can be a sharing of faith. The story of Ma Tshuma of Zimbabwe in the video recording, "Past Stories . . . Present Faith" (Mennonite Media Ministries), recounts her service for Christ following her rejection at the age of thirteen of the husband her father had chosen for her. That turning point led to her becoming acquainted with missionaries and becoming a traveling evangelist and church planter. Her story encourages viewers today to think about the turning points in their own lives.

Katie Funk Wiebe writes in *Bless Me Too, My Father* that stories show how the teller causes values to become living truth in another time and setting. "Without the story, preaching and teaching seem just so much pressure to conform to group beliefs." She continues, "An authentic story makes it impossible to pass off a string of words as the essence of the redeemed life. Above all, it passes on to one's children not an empty bucket, but shows them where to find the well."

Following a biblical pattern. To tell one's own story is to put oneself in the mode of the biblical pattern of storytelling. The Old Testament is the drama of God's people. The Israelites retold the story of the Exodus, the wilderness wandering, and the conquest time after time. The New Testament is an account of Jesus' storytelling and of his story.

Sharing one's story with children, grandchildren, and friends is not a little exercise to fill time. It is a way of showing that we, too, are in the line of God's history with the specifics of how, who, what and its meaning to us.

A review of your past could lead young people to "a reassessment of their values—values that may have been sidestepped and overlooked because no one pointed them out. You can help to identify to a new generation the past acts of God in your life, so that those looking for evidence of God's working today can recognize it in a new social setting" (Katie Funk Wiebe, *Good Times with Old Times: How to Write Your Memoirs*).

"Memoirs provide a unique outlook that helps establish a family identity, a foundation that can influence that family for years to come," is Patricia Ann Case's word in *How to Write Your Own Autobiography*.

It helps if young people carry images in their minds of the way another generation dreamt and made promises to God, to church and to society, and of the way they risked, sometimes failed, sometimes succeeded in these promises, says Wiebe.

On the last page of Dostoevsky's novel, *The Brothers Karamazov*, Alyosha says, "You must know that there is nothing higher and stronger and more wholesome and good for life in the future than some good memory, especially a memory of childhood, of home."

Psychologically healing. Psychologists speak of a life review, a thinking through one's life, as an important activity for the mental health of older adults. Robert N. Butler writes that in life review older adults are not only "taking stock of themselves as they review their lives, they are trying to think and feel through what they will do with the time that is left and with whatever emotional and material legacies they may have to give to others" (*Why Survive? Being Old in America*).

Evelyn Eaton Whitehead and James D. Whitehead concur. They agree that an increasing interest in one's past in the mature years is "important and developmentally sound." Through recollecting, reliving, and storytelling, older adults achieve acceptance of their own past. Pulling together the memories of the past is a way of bringing the loose ends together and acknowledging: "This is my life. This is the way it will have to be." Butler speaks of the process of life review as "a natural healing process" of unresolved conflicts and vague goals for whatever period is left in life.

HOW TO BEGIN

Much storytelling takes the form of reminiscing when family and friends get together. It is often spontaneous, unselective, and highly informal. Some stories may never be completed; others told two and three times, to the dismay of listeners. At other times younger family members come to grandparents with a set of questions about the "olden days." But the stories, short or long, fulfill a need of the speaker to leave a memory behind for posterity.

Cornelia Lehn writes of storytelling, "All the members of my family told stories, so it just never occurred to me that I would not be able to tell them. That was fortunate. Maybe if nobody knew they could not, everybody would tell stories and fill the world with beauty and meaning."

While writing is one of the most popular forms of preserving one's story, also consider using a audio- or videotape recorder. Work from notes or have someone interview you, using a set of questions to keep the memory pump primed.

If you plan to preserve your memories in a more systematic way, begin by recalling one small memory from any time or place in your life:

"The day I was born . . . " (Of course, you don't remember, but you were there and someone may still remember.)

"The first day of school . . ."

"The day I left home . . ."

The journey can begin anywhere. It is one where you can linger along the way—or speed up. There will be parts of your life that will be more fruitful in memories. Some persons remember very little of their early life. One man, writing his story, wrote ten typewritten pages of the first five years of his life. Another had only a half dozen clear memories.

Christopher de Vinck, essayist, writes, "As we grow older we tend to focus our attention upon those things we trusted and believed in when we were children. We just have to know where to find them."

You won't run out of stories to tell. Flannery O'Connor once suggested that anyone who has survived childhood knows enough about life to write for the rest of life. But you will have to keep reminding yourself, "I am giving a part of myself as a gift." It will make it worthwhile, for giving gifts is one of life's deepest pleasures.

WHAT TO SHARE

Most older persons' stories focus on three broad categories: the typical life cycle events, crises, and personal values. These might include births and deaths, illnesses, and migrations. They also include historical events—wars and revolutions, the Great Depression, rapid social and cultural change, and the person's experience in them. The area of personal values includes life-changing experiences and life philosophy, including spiritual experiences and theological change, child rearing, human sexuality, and church ministry.

To find information, ask yourself questions: How did your family celebrate special events and holidays? What were the rituals of life that gave your family stability? What have you carried over from your growing-up family life to the present? Were there patterns that you deliberately discarded? What did you enlarge or add? What were some turning points in your life? What were the stages in your faith journey?

Talk to persons who shared your life.

At a family gathering one woman taped up sheets of newsprint all around the meeting room. Each sheet had a date on it. During the weekend family members wrote in events they remembered for particular years.

The goal at all times is to share a whole life. Your life is more than a series of biological events. In the process of those events, you were becoming the person you are. That is the richness of your life.

The year I turned seventy I kept a daily journal recording how it felt to be seventy. Reading it later, I found that parts of it were dry as dust, even to me, the chief character. That happened when I left out the "feeling" words, the backbone of all meaningful writing—words like "I cried when..., I love..., I wondered..., I wish..., I was sad when...."

Be sure to name people. If they were important in your past, they deserve a place in your story. They also add interest to your story.

IF YOU CAN'T REMEMBER

Trying to recall an event, particularly one shared with a family member, will raise the question, "Do I remember it clearly?" After I had written the account of a disastrous rabbit-raising project I had shared with my brother, I gave him the story. He added and corrected. "Don't you remember?" he asked regarding our burgeoning industry, details I had forgotten or deliberately blocked out.

But, of course, we are both right. What we both remember is the truth as we perceived it.

So bring out anything that can jog your memory. My old spelling book covered with scraps of oilcloth from our summer kitchen table can transport me back to my Illinois childhood with speed that outclasses a jet.

Bring out the photographs, old letters, old diaries.

Draw some pictures, the floor plan of the house where you grew up—the table at home with circles for each person around it when you were twelve. Color each person, not hair and eye coloring, but how the personality seemed to you. I color my brother, two years younger than myself, orange because he was always lively. I color my father deep brown for his sturdy reliability.

There are times when there is only one place to go for verification and doing so seems important. One story writer traveled across country to visit the homestead and the graves of her grandparents she had never known.

Another called her brother who had enlisted in the army when she was a child at home. She remembered it as a painful time for her pacifist parents. In all the years since then she and her brother had not talked about it. She called her brother in another state and found him glad to talk about his decision, about his life in the army, and how it had changed his life. For both of them it was a healing time.

Through the years I have spoken or written about not having had a public library card when I was growing up in the country six miles from Sterling, Illinois. We were off limits for free library service, even though it was (is) an Andrew Carnegie library with "Free to all people" over the front door. For me, passing that library was a little like arriving at the gate of heaven and facing a "No Trespassing" sign.

I thought it odd that we did not have a card, since my parents put education high on their list of priorities, even though both had limited formal schooling. Was it too expensive to buy a card?

Finally, forty-five years later, I called from Pennsylvania to Illinois to the library and asked, "How much did a library card cost in 1932?"

The answering voice hesitated just a moment in surprise and then said, "If you will hold, I will go check." After a considerable hold she returned and said, "One dollar for three months."

Then I understood. I did not delude myself into thinking that it was a small fee for a card. That was Depression time with corn prices so low that it didn't pay to truck corn to a grain elevator. After that phone call that cost more than a half year's worth of a library card in 1932, I knew why we didn't have a card.

Just as in one's spiritual life there are "dark nights of the soul," there will be times of serious doubts about what you are doing. Is this sharing about your life of any earthly good to anyone? Are you telling the truth? Are you able to tell the truth even if it is unpleasant? (Yes, to preserve only the favorable is propaganda.) Can you recall the sad times of life and live through their pain again?

Do you have the energy to think about your own life and share it in writing or to use a tape recorder week after week? And there is always the nagging fear, "Can I say it in such a way that it's worth doing?" It is in such times that a firm goal helps to lead the person toward the Goal.

HUMOR MAKES THE ROAD LESS BUMPY

As you dig into your past to share what is significant, you will be tempted to preach or teach, to want to moralize. Remind yourself that you are a storyteller and the value of your life will come out in what you write without special emphasis.

Reviewing your own story is serious work. But remember that there were light moments in your life, too. Humor makes the road less bumpy. Someone has said "If people are too grouchy too long, they don't get old. They die." Humor writer Tom Mullen adds, "Laughter in, around, or in spite of grief is an affirmation that death itself is not final."

An increasing number in the medical profession are beginning to recognize the physical healing power of humor. In several retirement homes, elderly residents take regular humor "medicine"—funny books, poems, cartoons, movies and performances by stand-up comedians, reports Tal D. Bonham in *Humor: God's Gift.*

Florida Scott Maxwell kept a journal the year she was eighty-two. She wrote: "My kitchen linoleum is so black and shiny that I waltz while I wait for the kettle to boil. This pleasure is for the old who live alone. No matter how old a mother is she watches her middle-aged children for signs of improvement. When a new disability arrives I look about to see if death has come, and I call quietly, 'Death is that you? Are you there?' So far the disability has answered, 'Don't be silly, it's me.'"

JOURNAL WRITING

Another useful resource for the older adult interested in recording memories is journal writing. Even if you only begin now, it will serve you well for recording the present and stimulating memories.

To keep a journal is to write "instant autobiography." It is best if it is a record of inner and outer weather. It is not meant

to be an account of what happened on a certain day: "Went to
town . . . ate at The Maples . . . had the roast beef dinner . . ."
(although such events are part of the day). Rather, a journal is
a gathering up of what one enjoyed, thought, or feared.
Journal writing has to do with emotions, attitudes, and moods.

Honesty is the goal of such writing—not an easy task,
especially in matters of the inner life. Jesus said, "The kingdom of God is within you." That is, God is present in each
day's living. Salvation history is also found in the story of
our own inner lives.

A journal helps one to see, to really see. It keeps one from
thinking that there is anything commonplace. Ira Proghoff,
long-time journal teacher, says, "When you use the journal
you're saying, 'I need a time of reflection, of quieting. I need a
sabbath.'" The need for rest after activity is a sound principle.
A journal is a way to create one's own personal Sabbath.

Dora Wilson, a Quaker, in *The Journal and the Journey,*
writes, "It's like a woman [or a man] with two pockets. The
left pocket is full of a tangle of string. In the right pocket is
a small ball of neatly wound string. When the woman has
time and feels like it, she takes out the tangle and winds a
piece of it onto the ball and slowly the tangle gets smaller
and the ball gets larger." Going back over your life journey
allows you to take the rough spots, the times of conflict, the
long-held grudges and untangle them in your mind.

The most common form of journaling is *crisis-related,*
like an illness, death, loss of job or friend, economic distress, emotional depression. This kind of journaling is a
therapeutic lifeline when one is floundering at sea and
needs to be rescued. But such a journal will probably not
record the joys and triumphs, the insights that are an
important part of life.

Another kind of journal is *portrait journaling.* This is a
recording of day-by-day thoughts—of what you believe, how
you deal with life's experiences, with some thought given to
the major themes of your life.

The portrait journal is for your eyes alone. Its value is
in the freedom with which you can write when you have

provided yourself with a level of privacy. Without such a safeguard, consciously or unconsciously, you will censor what you write and sacrifice honesty.

Older persons need to make the deposition of their journals and writing clear in their will or other instructions to family members. Are they to be destroyed or kept?

Later the portrait journal can be edited and formed into a *legacy journal*, the writings you want to leave as a gift to those you care about.

A legacy journal is for the future. You will consider carefully what you want to include from your portrait journal. Parts that might be harmful to others or yourself after your death will not be included. Parts that are intimate and appropriate in a portrait journal may be unsuitable for a legacy journal you hope your family members will read.

Ask: Was this common knowledge at the time it happened? Did it affect a large group of people? Will it build friendship or will it destroy? Is it important to tell it or is this something that had best be forgotten?

Because a legacy journal is valuable for those who follow you, you may even want to designate money in your will to have it published and stipulate who will get copies.

A form of a legacy journal is *letter-writing*. For the past fifteen years columnist James J. Kilpatrick has written an annual birthday letter to his grandchild, Heather. "I write to preserve a few remembered whens for both of us. A long time ago I concluded that love, the kind of love that lasts, is mostly an accumulation of remembered whens."

"For everything there is a season, and a time for every matter under heaven," wrote the Preacher in Ecclesiastes 3:1 (RSV). The years when daily work demands are less may be the time to think of sharing your story in some form.

What are the events, thoughts, feelings, relationships, experiences that you want your family, friends, and church family to be aware of from your life? Who but you has the material? It is your legacy for those following you in life. What a gift you have to give!

To think and talk about

1. The tendency to reminisce is sometimes seen as a sign of old age. Robert N. Butler sees it as a normal process, the act of putting one's life in order and acceptance of the life cycle. What do you think?

2. Is it not possible that thinking through the past may bring about sadness and depression because of previous mismanaged and unwise decisions? What is the best approach to dealing with a difficult past?

3. One older woman states, "My children don't want to hear about the past, especially the difficult times. They think I am laying a guilt trip on them because they are enjoying a much higher standard of living." How can younger adults be encouraged to listen?

4. Some congregations have regular times of sharing stories. Does your church provide such a setting? Consider starting one.

5. Family reunions are great places to share memories. Some people stay away because of this; others enjoy the stories. What skills are needed for good storytelling?

In some congregations ministry is often seen as something done to the elderly, in particular making sure their physical needs are met. More recently this emphasis has shifted to ministry with the elderly. As they are able, older people are encouraged to continue to contribute in whatever capacity they can. This chapter focuses on a third approach, while not denying the validity of the first two: learning from the older person.

Older persons have rich and varied contributions to make of wisdom and insights from former leadership roles and other types of experiences, and as examples of positive attitudes toward life. Does this learning from the older person take place formally? informally? Laban and Helen Peachey tell us what they have learned from older persons.

CHAPTER 12

OLDER PERSONS: OUR ROLE MODELS IN THE ART OF LIVING

Laban and Helen Peachey

How should we live as years roll by? How do we draw on the experiences of others? What should we be looking for? These questions are old and simple, but society has made the answers hard and complex.

"How do you draw on the experiences of older adults to balance out your life?" I asked Ken Garber, fifty-two. He pondered awhile. "There's no way I can reach a balance at this stage of my life," he said. "I try to balance things out over several decades."

Ken and Doris are busy people. He is a former college teacher turned businessman who often works six days a week and sometimes part of seven. Doris is in management and lives an intense life of her own. They know in their heads that life will change for them in fifteen to twenty years, but they cannot grasp emotionally what form those changes will take. They want the whole of life to balance out. If their business and professional efforts pay off, they should be able to retire early and make up for their present over-time with a more relaxed lifestyle.

Hectic and *pressed* are words that describe the Garbers' work schedule. They are surviving, but also having fun. Learning from older persons is not a conscious priority for them, at least not now.

In a way, the Garbers are typical of many middle-aged people. Business, family, unplanned crises, and some recreation take up most available time and energy. Church activities and responsibilities are part of this intense lifestyle. Much of their time and energy is a response to commitments and patterns established one, two, or even three decades ago, some of which they learned from older adults.

Parents of infants and toddlers do not schedule "talking lessons" for them. Children pick up whatever language and accent their parents and friends use because they are members of a language community. Feral children (children who grow up in the wild without human contact) do not learn to use language.

Similarly, even though people do not talk about it directly, children, young adults, and middle-aged people like the Garbers learn "the language of growing older" if they are part of a community that includes young and old. Grandchildren learn that older people can be a lot of fun, or that they can be grumpy bears, unhappy with life. They learn that death is part of the life cycle. Consciously or unconsciously, younger persons sense how older people use their time, establish their values and priorities, and how they move into retirement.

Ken's comment that he and Doris look at "life as a whole" gave Helen and me a clue that people moving along the age ladder are planning for the future. They are learning from older adults, not in scheduled class sessions with papers and tests, but by watching them in their family, congregation, and community. The test comes when they themselves become part of the older generation.

ARE THERE MODELS FOR GROWING OLDER?

As Helen and I moved toward age sixty, we asked people just older than ourselves, "How should we live between sixty and ninety? How should we prepare? Is this period a good time?"

The responses to our questions were varied, sometimes opposites. I asked two men, one seventy-four and one eighty, what advice they would give a sixty-five-year-old. One said, "Turn your assets into cash and then travel." The other said, "It is better stewardship to give your assets to the church. I don't want to travel."

What older adults said to us indicated that many of them do not work carefully and systematically at ordering their lives. One man said, "We live about as we did before." After studying this couple, we concluded that in their young and middle years their external environment had directed them how to live. They never took charge of their own lives. So, of course, they lived much the same way after retirement.

We also observed many wonderful examples of persons for whom the last one third of life is certainly the richest, the most fruitful, and the best. Who are these people? *Gracious, joyful* and *positive* are words that best describe many of them. They are people of "The Book." Their lifestyle and attitude are shaped by cultivating the fruit of the Spirit (Gal. 5:22-23). They know who they are and what they believe, but they make room for others who differ. They live to give, serve, and support. They also exhibit a capacity to adapt to external changes.

The oldest people among us have experienced a wide range of social and technical changes in this century. They have lived from the horse-drawn buggy to the moon buggy, from the Marxist revolution to the demise of the Russian Communist state. By the way they have adapted to these changes, these people are teaching the next generation. For some, the mind or the body wears out, making life difficult. In a word, they have undergone the full range of human experience. Their lives are filled with both joys and sorrows. What lessons do they teach us?

HOW TO MAINTAIN A POSITIVE ATTITUDE AND GENTLE SPIRIT

Florence was an early missionary doctor and married a missionary widower she met in India. Mina was a mother of small children when her husband, also a missionary, died in India. Then Florence's husband died. We learned to know Florence and Mina when they were both living in a retirement home. They enjoyed talking about their years in India, but they lived much in the present and were especially concerned about young people, college students, and their own grandchildren.

At church, Mina, almost blind, would shake my hand and say, "Brother Peachey, I am praying for you." The next week I might receive a check for Hesston College, of which I was president at the time, with a penciled note stating, "This is what I have left this month from my Social Security."

Others will remember Florence and Mina for their missionary service, but we remember them for their pleasant attitude, wholesome spirit, and gentle disposition. Some people become unhappy or bitter when they encounter difficult experiences. Florence and Mina became more generous, trusting, and prayerful. They were genuinely interested in other people. Their lives were enriched by a lifetime of unselfish caring for others. Commitments of faith reaching deep in their souls shaped the essence of their lives. They naturally grew into positive, gentle, and happy persons. Helen and I want to achieve the same as we grow older.

HOW TO REMAIN GRACIOUSLY TOLERANT

Life in the military is not a likely preparation for membership in a traditional Mennonite congregation. Harold and Bettie met while each pursued a military career during World War II. They returned to civilian life, raised a family, and enjoyed successful careers, Bettie in cancer research and Harold in education. As they moved toward retirement, the church and the fellowship of Christians became their first priority. They have found a church to unite with and a group of Christians to fellowship with within that congregation from which they draw spiritual strength. But they also make a major spiritual contribution to the congregation. They have held church offices and responsibilities, such as teaching Sunday school, but their major impact has been through their personal, informal concern for the welfare of others and their godly presence.

Does membership in a Mennonite church and in the Pentagon establishment create conflict? During the Persian Gulf War we asked Harold and Bettie, over Sunday dinner, "How do you integrate the diverse experiences or components of your lives?"

Their military careers are a reality of their young adult years, a part of who they are. Yet their spiritual pilgrimage led them to a deep faith and meaningful fellowship among a people that takes seriously the Sermon on the Mount in the face of the 1991 Desert Storm. In grappling with these issues, Harold and Bettie stand firm in placing their first loyalty to God and God's sovereign will. The story of their pilgrimage showed me a gracious tolerance that inspires in a world of conflict and confusion.

People who know Harold and Bettie have a clear sense that they live close to God and carry on an extensive ministry of intercession. While the local congregation is important to them, they also maintain a wider spiritual fellowship and communication network.

Linden and Esther's background is vastly different from Harold and Bettie's background. In his younger years, Linden pastored a rural, mountain congregation. After graduate work, he became a college and seminary teacher, and spent twenty-five years in church administration as a bishop. Esther spent two years in public school teaching and twenty-four more in a private high school, mostly as librarian. Though each was a professional, they enjoyed working together in the church. During a lifetime of more than seventy-five years, they both gained churchwide experience and rarely missed a church conference. Linden says, "As we have grown older, we are more relaxed and find it easier to look at things from other people's point of view. Since I am not teaching or working as a bishop, I have learned to see the lighter side of life and the humor in many situations."

Linden and Esther were a part of the Mennonite church fifty years ago when the bishops regulated members' lives strictly. Now they are happy in a different type of church setting, even saying many of the changes are for the better. Their faith is not threatened by fellowship with persons whose point of view and experience are different from theirs.

We learned much from these two couples: They live close to God, with disciplined and regular prayer lives. Their own convictions are clear and firmly in place. They have learned that diversity can become the means to enrich their own lives. Both couples find deep spiritual fellowship with persons on a wide spectrum of biblical interpretation.

Elton Trueblood has said, "Be tough on issues, but gentle with people." Here are two couples whose lives are firmly planted in the biblical expression of faith. They are interested in the cutting edge of the church and a wide range of activities in the larger church and community. As they sense what is constructive and contributes to the building of God's kingdom, they give it their energy and affirmation.

How to care for all God's children

Frances lives alone in the old farmhouse where she and her late husband raised a fine family of six children. Frances has known grief and tragedy. Her only son died in an auto accident. Her husband died ten years ago. Five daughters with their families live nearby. One son-in-law has operated the dairy farm since her husband's death.

We watch her, at age seventy-seven, walking stick in

hand, lead the herd of cows to pasture. She faithfully visits the sick, takes cookies or flowers to shut-ins, and instinctively knows who in the community needs a cheer-up visit. It is many years since Frances retired from teaching school, but she is still a regular substitute Sunday school teacher—any class, any age. At the nearby Church of the Brethren she continues to minister as a sort of spiritual mother to all. She is an associate for Wycliffe Bible Translators and gathers participants to attend the annual promotional dinner. Her house is the stopover for Wycliffe travelers. Hospitality is her gift whether guests come to her home or she goes to theirs. When we are her age, we hope to have compassionate hearts with good health and energy, to share our lives and home in a caring ministry of hospitality.

HOW TO MAKE TIME TO HELP OTHERS

Jesus taught the crowd on the mountainside, "Do not store up for yourselves treasures on earth . . . but store up for yourselves treasures in heaven" (Matt. 6:19,20, NIV). These words have become alive and practical for Helen and me as we've watched Ed and Orpha make time to help others for the past twenty years.

Ed and Orpha operated a modest business in a small rural Kansas community. To observers, their transition to retirement seemed easy. Over the years they had done voluntary service for several weeks or months at a time, so they sold their business to have more time to help others.

The six to eight years they spent in Ohio and Virginia in voluntary service were the best years of their lives. In addition to their service, they had time to be with children and grandchildren who lived in four states from Iowa to Virginia. This time together as a family was especially important to grown grandchildren, some of whom were college students. It drew the extended family together.

For years Ed suffered from a heart condition. With Orpha and the children he made funeral plans, realizing death could come at any time. One Sunday evening, after a wonderful day visiting friends, he died. Family, church family, and friends from far and wide gathered at the funeral to grieve, but also to celebrate with joy Ed's life and faith. He had planned his funeral service that way.

HOW TO LIVE UNTHREATENED BY CHANGE

John was a traditional Eastern farm boy. Milo was a pioneer from the Northern prairie. Though their lives and careers differed greatly, these two sons of the nineteenth century teach some great lessons about life.

John, a Virginian, was born in 1896. He lived along the same country road, now a highway, for ninety-six years. Milo moved by Conestoga wagon from northwest Missouri to the prairies of North Dakota in 1900 when he was two years old. Both men married, raised their families, and were a stable part of a Mennonite congregation throughout their lifetimes.

John spent his working years as a farmer and a dairy tester. He is also an accomplished cabinet maker and wood craftsman. He describes the grandfather clock he made at age ninety-four for a daughter as a lifetime masterpiece.

Milo was a college and seminary graduate, a remarkable accomplishment for the 1920s. He became a pastor, Bible teacher, and evangelist, and held the position of president of Hesston College and Bible School from 1932 to 1951. Working to assure the school's survival during the Depression was certainly a major achievement for him.

For both John and Milo their marriage partner played an important role in their lives. Both chose women of strong character, deeply supportive of their husband's work, yet following independent interests apart from those of their husband's.

Milo was able to get close to students even in the last years of his long life. In his mid-eighties he gave a chapel talk that was deeply moving and much appreciated by the student body and faculty. Soon after Milo's death, Keith Zehr, a Hesston College graduate and staff member, wrote about Brother Milo's amazing rapport with students and influence upon them. At the time there were some problems among the students. Zehr writes, "Yet I heard Milo mention none of these things. He talked about the great and wonderful opportunities our students had today. He mentioned that while some say Hesston College students are not as dedicated as they once were, he didn't believe that was true. 'More today than ever, we have students who are dedicated to serving their church and Jesus Christ,'" Milo said. He encouraged students to use their gifts to go out and make a difference in the world. "I believe this encouragement and affirmation was a key reason for the popularity of Milo Kauffman among the student body at Hesston College. I have to pause and ponder how many lives have been touched and changed by this man's caring attitude" (*Gospel Herald,* May 24, 1988).

John Wenger has much the same spirit. On Sunday morning he arrives at church a half hour early. He talks with many people before and after the service. He's interested in what people are thinking, gives encouragement, and shares ideas. Recently, the Sunday morning program included a number of out-of-the-ordinary activities. During sharing time, he said that in years gone by he could predict what would happen at each weekly service. Now every Sunday morning service was a surprise. "And I like it that way!" he said. At ninety-six he could adapt to change.

Milo and John may seem different, but we can learn much from them. They are clear about who they are and what they believe. They are at peace with themselves and can reach into the lives of others without experiencing personal threat. Affirmation, understanding, and encouragement are much more powerful influences on the younger generation than criticism.

Milo died at age ninety. John still has things he wants to accomplish and hopes to celebrate his one hundredth birthday in 1996! As these two men grew older, they continued active involvement, contributing to the life of the local congregation. Each congregation made room for and respected the unique contribution that Milo and John brought from their century of experience.

HOW TO TURN THE OLDER YEARS INTO THE WONDER YEARS

Helen and I have met many people in the past two decades for whom the older years are truly a time of wonder. One man said, "It's like being a child again with time to explore, sense, and feel." He spoke of the carefree happiness of his childhood enriched by a half century of adult experience.

Each year in August about one hundred adults gather at Laurelville Church Center, Laurelville, Pennsylvania, for fellowship, Bible study, meeting friends, and sharing life. The week takes on an air of excitement and wonder as people share hobbies and exhibit the products of new or old skills they now have time to develop and enjoy. This annual event is a beautiful expression of the psalmist: "The righteous . . . will still bear fruit in old age, they will stay fresh and green, proclaiming, 'The Lord is upright; he is my Rock . . .'" (Ps. 92:12-15, NIV).

The people we have met at these gatherings of older adults are unique persons. Their individuality is often accentuated by experience. Older people with a lifetime of creativity and experience are a distinct idiom and can only be understood by careful listening.

HOW TO MOVE FROM INDEPENDENT TO DEPENDENT LIVING

Most older people live in their own homes, but some have moved to nursing homes. We have learned equally from both groups. Those in nursing homes must make many adjustments—especially from independence to dependency. These are people who have lost some of the control of their own lives. Other people schedule meals, bedtime, baths, and many other daily activities. Physical and/or mental limitations necessitate new ways of relating to their families. When people experience losses, their need for love and caring is greater. A touch, a hug, and time to talk are meaningful to them. Their response may be a smile, a "God bless you," a pulling away, or no response at all.

As Robert's health failed, Sara cared for him at home as long as she could. After he moved into the nursing home, Sara sat with her husband each day to feed him and care for his personal needs. Robert enjoyed visitors even though he could not converse, so Sara carried on the conversation. Toward the end of his life, Robert often called out in an embarrassing manner, but Sara came faithfully every day. Being at his bedside constantly was not easy for her, and she became weary. Her children helped her decide to take one day off each week to be at home.

Twenty-five years ago Kate's husband, James, began acting abnormally. He was a minister, a public school teacher, a pleasant person, loved by many. His wife was a good partner in his activities. She cared for him in their home until her health was jeopardized and his Alzheimer's-like behavior made it necessary to transfer him to a safer place.

James and Kate are both in their eighties. In many ways, James is like a young child, with limited response to his surroundings. Yet Kate comes faithfully several times each week to be with him. She brings her tatting along, visits with his friends that stop by, and sometimes James sings a song with her.

Half a century ago Sara and Kate did not know what the promise "for better or for worse" would mean for them. But their love was strong enough to survive the "worse" times. Each woman cared for her husband at home as long as she could, and then, with the support of her family, decided to place him in a nursing home so that she could care for her own needs.

Faithfulness to a spouse, even when that spouse is severely incapacitated, is a powerful example to others at a time when partners are discarded because they no longer bring fulfillment to the marriage. Every time a couple celebrates a golden wedding anniversary, it speaks of forgiveness, forbearance, and love.

Being grateful for those who pick up the burden of caring for a loved one when you can't is another lesson in the grace of adaptability.

Young people and middle-aged persons gain wisdom by trying to understand what makes some older people live out their lives like a smoothly flowing stream despite the numerous hazards of the journey. What experiences or events shaped their outlook? In responding to one of his friends who came to comfort him in his misery, Job says: "Does not the ear test words as the tongue tastes food? Is not wisdom found among the aged? Does not long life bring understanding?" (Job 12:11,12, NIV).

Helen and I found that as older people talk about how their lives unfolded, they reveal a deep reverence for God's providence in what happened over the years and in present events. The variety of their past experiences prepared them for the mystery of the unexpected. They often show a freedom to respond to God's Spirit in ways they could not have enjoyed during their working years. This freedom leads to new experiences, new thinking, and new understandings of the ways God relates to humanity.

The church that discovers older people as a resource in the art of living discovers an inexhaustible supply.

TO THINK AND TALK ABOUT

1. Think of older people in your church and community who have taught you something valuable. Share your learnings with the group.

2. In order to learn from older people, young and old need opportunities to spend time together. How is this brought about in your congregation? in your family? What can be done to bring the older generation and children closer together?

3. Church voluntary service is a popular form of service for older people. Some of them travel to other states and even to other countries. Others minister in their home communities. Have someone who has been involved in such service share their experiences with you. What kind of voluntary service do you look forward to doing some day?

4. Why are some older people unthreatened by change? Many, in fact, look forward to new ideas and ways

of doing things. How is such an open attitude developed in younger people?

5. Elbert C. Cole, a staunch advocate of older people, has said, "The future of the church is in the hands of older adults, not young people." Do you agree or disagree?

6. He also said, "Young people see our ability or inability to make life come alive in the later years" and model themselves after us. What do you think he means by "coming alive in the later years"?

During 1991 Paul M. Miller interviewed seventy-four eighty-year-old residents of three retirement homes in Lancaster County, Pennsylvania. The residents were selected by the retirement home chaplains as persons able to reflect wisely about the place of hope in their lives. After several weeks advance notice, Miller asked them to trace how the hopes they had felt as small children were tested or modified by their experiences during the next seventy years, and then to summarize their hopes now at age eighty. These seventy-four respondents (thirty-seven females and thirty-seven males), represented nine denominations, many professions, and many levels of physical functioning. Seven had never married, forty were grandparents, and fifteen were great-grandparents. All had been active workers in their congregations, one as a deacon and three as pastors. Miller shares what he learned from the wisdom of these eighty-year-olds about hope.

CHAPTER 13

AGING WITH HOPE IN THE FAITH COMMUNITY

Paul M. Miller

Whether young or old, human beings cannot live without hope. Yet an amazing silence about hope exists in crucial literature of the church. The hymnals used in Christian retirement homes have a much briefer list of hymns on the subject of hope than on faith and love! An equally astounding silence exists in the indexes of many popular and systematic theologies. Many otherwise thorough books on theology on my shelf simply omit the word *hope* in their indexes. Even scholarly journals, like *Generations,* Journal of the American Society of Aging, includes almost no reports about the hopes of Christian aged.

What is hope? Daniel J. Simundson in *Hope for All Seasons* defines hope as both a noun and verb. As a noun it includes the various things people hope for: the necessities of life, protection from danger, justice, community, and life after death. As a verb it means to "trust in the God who will walk with you into the unknown future."

A popular notion persists that during infancy and early childhood middle-class Americans hope for food, fun, friends, family, adventure, safety, growth, and status. But what does life do to these childish hopes? Hopes change as we move through life. As "hopers" grow older and survive what life brings to them, "hopes" become the verb "to hope." They move beyond looking for security in their human family to security in God's family in heaven. Older Christians hope that the image of God in their inner being will transcend their approaching death and continue to live on in their resurrected selves.

Though not much has been written about older persons' hopes, these people are traveling through life hopefully. The seventy-four older persons I interviewed offer fellow travelers seven suggestions to keep hope strong as they move with the seasons of life.

RECLAIM THE HOPES YOU WERE BORN WITH

Anna, a seventy-one-year-old woman, was an answer to her parents' prayers for a child. Her earliest memories are of family songs of praise. As a very young child, she knew her parents wanted her and that God loved her.

Like Anna, almost all the eighty-year-olds praised their mothers for their quiet optimism, constant loving availability, forgiving grace, and reverence with which they explained God's love as they told Bible stories. The eyes of the storytellers became moist as they told how sacredly their mother had carried an infant in her womb, given birth, nursed it, and taught it. Their mothers taught them (below the level of speech) to trust God through their own life of trust.

Ernest, more than ninety years old, said that he, too, like John the Baptist, had "leaped with joy" in his mother's womb! He insisted that God the Creator was constantly in his mother's mind as God formed his body and mind in the womb. His sustaining hope was the hope with which he was born.

Unfortunately, fathers were seldom mentioned by the seventy-four elderly as shapers of their hopes. Dads were described as "busy in the world of work," "not there when I went to sleep or awake," "important but distant," "big and strong but almost to be feared," "the boss of my mother." Fathers did not read Bible stories to them as children. Fathers did not invite them to bring their questions to them. Fathers did not remind them that God was someone like themselves, a "father."

Many interviewees drew a blank when they searched their memories for early impressions of their fathers. Some defended their father as "a good dad," highly honored in business, neighborhood, and profession, but unavailable to them when they were being formed as a person.

Roger, a seventy-eight-year-old, remembered that he had been baptized at the altar of God by God's priest and reared in a home where no one was allowed to use God's name in vain. His parents read from the New Testament to the family every night and always answered the children's questions. His father led table prayers. He remembers him expressing hope that the perilous times of these last days would end with the return of the Prince of Peace. His mother calmed the children's fears during thunderstorms. She taught child evangelism classes. Clearly, this man developed with a unique hope shaped by his parents.

The advice of these older persons was to reclaim the hope in Jesus Christ that their parents had given their children.

BE OPEN TO UNDESERVED GRACE THROUGHOUT LIFE

Almost all of the respondents, as they told their life-and-hope stories, expressed surprise at "inbreakings" of divine grace. At times God helped a good thing to happen. Sometimes hope broke through near despair. Many recited a tragedy that turned out better than they had hoped for through a providential circumstance, told of a remarkable escape from an accident, a quick recovery from an injury, or a "voice" that called and guided during a time of decision. Several said that repeatedly they felt as if they had a guardian angel watching over them, and could describe such an angel. They had experienced God's help in the past. God would continue to help in the future. That was their hope!

Ernest, eighty-one, told, with tears, of an uncle who gave him a nickel one day when their whole family was without food during the Great Depression. He bought a loaf of bread with that nickel, and that day his family ate! Rachel, seventy-six, a retired teacher, was "strong-willed and wild" as a child, but when her mother died when Rachel was eight and her father when she was thirteen, God came near. "I can never explain it, but it was oh, so real," she said.

Ada, seventy-seven-year-old widow, had hoped to be a mother and teacher. Many little miracles enabled her to go to college and be certified as a teacher. Then, with an equal sense of God's continuing grace in her life, she discovered first that she was sterile, later that she had cancer. She adopted children, who turned out well and gave her rewarding motherhood and now grandmotherhood.

Lee, seventy-nine, had a father who scolded him repeatedly: "You botched that again." As a child Lee regarded himself as a failure. Then, God's healing love gave him a new start after that early wreck. A new job gave him another chance after bankruptcy. Grace intervened when he was told to leave the mission field. He says, "I know that God will supply the grace for any need I face in my future."

The clear message of these older persons was to expect the unexpected breakthroughs of God's grace even as a young person. Such undeserved grace increases hope. Hope is always a gift of God, not something you can drum up.

IF YOU WANT TO LIVE WITH HOPE, BE FAITHFUL TO GOD

Twenty-nine of the seventy-four storytellers told of definite decisions to be faithful to God. At specific times they had said yes to a specific call from God. In the midst of a crisis, in which they were tempted to give up hope altogether, they took a quiet step of faith in desperation. They joyfully recounted times when they persisted in following Jesus Christ even though their decision was a costly one. For these aged pilgrims, sowing and reaping was a law of life. "Sow in faithfulness if you want to reap hopefulness," they inferred. For them hope was a decision. They decided again and again, whether they always felt hopeful or not, to set their hopes in the living God and God's justice and grace.

Charles, one hundred, was jeered in the men's dormitory at the prestigious college he attended when he recommitted his life to Christ. In this crisis he learned "to reach out and to touch Christ personally, almost as the early disciples touched his garments." This decisive act of faith changed his life and outlook.

Renee, eighty-three, held onto hope during a massive "nervous breakdown," which forced her to quit teaching school here in America. She kept on in faithful and loving service overseas, although in a low-key role. There new Christians renewed and deepened her hope. She married for the first time at age seventy-eight and continues to hope in all areas of her life.

Three aged men told stories of the hardship of being "hired out" as a child after one or both parents died. Although forced to do chores in the barn at 4:30 a.m., they worked faithfully, even though they felt so worthless they used the smelly outhouse instead of the inside bathroom. Finally, their employers rewarded their faithfulness with loving esteem, almost as if they were a son rather than a despised "hired boy."

Mabel, seventy-four, listed the greatest tests of her faithfulness. She found catechism classes dull and boring, but she didn't quit attending. Her father died when she was seventeen, but she did not give up hope. Her husband lost his job during the Depression and the family suffered hunger. Her husband dropped dead in the snow one winter day and she became depressed. But by being faithful to God in each test, she became more hopeful that she will triumph whatever may come her way.

Randy, eighty-two, advised that he has Alzheimer's disease and may not have long to live, said reverently, "The Lord is preparing me, through my physical condition, to turn my mind heavenward. I will use every opportunity for Christian witness." He is committed to remaining faithful to the end inasmuch as he is able to control his mind.

These older people rely upon God's image within them and trust in a liberating God. They expect God's providential love. They believe that God suffers with them in their pain, and God's Son walks ahead of them, preparing a way for them into the future. Yet, they acknowledge they need to claim their union with the Life-giver in faith.

These aged all have in common a very personal piety. They recognize they need to follow Christ like a child and to adventure into the prayer closet and be alone with God. They choose to live already in the reality of eternity. They have learned to endure many small deaths to self if resurrection power is to be theirs. God provides their daily manna, but they have to go out and gather it. When they make God their Alpha every day, God becomes their Omega.

YOU NEED TWO KINDS OF FAMILIES TO MAINTAIN HOPE

As the elderly traced the pattern of hope in the story of their lives, they usually found hope grew stronger because of two kinds of families: a biological family and a faith family. All were sure that their present marriage would last, since they had remained true to one another so long. All were confident that their congregation (their faith family) loved them very much. Their two families kept them from feeling marginalized, lonely, valueless, and helpless.

Many of these respondents seemed surprised at their children's love for them. Their adult children, deeply involved in caring for their own children, still rallied around them. More than ever before, they realized that they are loved for who they are.

Tensions between generations that had developed over the years faded and were replaced with love in both family and congregational life. Letters, cards, phone calls and contacts miraculously increased in number. Children newly affirmed family values and valued heirlooms. Prodigals were welcomed home. The congregation began to provide special caring and fellowship focused on their needs.

Especially gratifying and surprising to many of these elderly were their grandchildren's love and concern. Apparently, some parents were teaching their youth to cherish family systems. Alma, an eighty-one-year-old grandmother, chuckled as she said, "There must be some hope for a good future because my grandchildren are just grand."

Bernice, ninety-six, placed her relationship with her twelve grandchildren and great-grandchildren above every other joy and satisfaction in life. "Just as my grandpa brought warm food to school for my lunch when I was seven, so now I live for my twelve," she said. "My daughters call me every week. My twelve took me out to Mt. Gretna to dinner for Christmas. All of my twelve love me very much. I pray for my twelve by name every day. They are part of my hope for the future."

Unfortunately such love and respect from young people is not equally true in their congregations. These interviewees wistfully admitted that they barely know the church youth. "They grow up so fast," "I don't even know their names," they said.

However, not all family contacts were pleasant. Frank, eighty, was heartbroken because he felt forced to cancel his family's plans to celebrate Christmas in his apartment. He said, in tears, "Those little kids, with their fighting and noise, just get to me. I can't stand it anymore, no matter how I try. I'm afraid they all think I don't love them."

Without prompting, fully one-half of the aged telling their life stories and hopes spoke a good word for their experience of church and family life in their retirement home. They particularly valued the availability of the chaplain, the protection of their privacy, and the familiarity of the worship. They appreciated the caring staff, excellent medical care, and opportunity for small Bible study and prayer groups. They noted the beauty of their environment, and in a few cases, the delicious food and the recreation suited to their level of strength. One chaplain was emphatic in calling residents "a family" and spoke often of "our family life," "our family concerns," and "our family sharing."

HOPE MAINTAINS ITSELF WHEN PEACEMAKING IS A GOAL

The elderly who live in these three retirement centers have learned that the gift of the years can heal the hurts of the years. They seemed to have fully forgiven pastors and parents for their partial failures in an earlier time. They have corrected childish misconceptions about how perfect parents and pastors must be. They mentioned how their parents had made them feel secure. Often their earliest teachers made them feel like persons of worth by giving prime time to listening to their childish fears and hopes.

This group of elderly people sometimes set out deliberately to forgive persons they wish they had forgiven long ago. To go on holding a grudge was no longer worth the pain and loneliness it brought. Arguments in earlier years now seemed petty, wrong, or stupid. The wisdom of the years helped these elderly persons to see the error of their ways. Many were able to humbly repent, admit they had been mistaken, and to announce a change of mind.

Several said they were glad our church leaders were "apologizing to the American Indians, to blacks, to immigrants, and anyone our systems have abused."

War in the Middle East was either looming or raging during the time these elderly were being interviewed. These men and women were a group of people from various denominations who longed for peace in the world. Only one person defended war as "a necessary path to peace." No one claimed Desert Storm was a just war. With quiet passion many told of their private prayers to God for world peace.

The interviewees seemed reflective as they expressed their hope to actually do something for world peace. Probably one person in five spoke of some peacemaking effort they were involved in with the family, retirement home, neighborhood, church, world. Some sent money to help a peacemaking cause.

Ted, seventy-nine, spoke with quiet passion about his prayer for peace. He said, "Although I lack the strength to work for peace with all the available methods now, God will continue to empower me to write letters, call my congressman, pray, plead, protest, or in some way be a peacemaker." During his lifetime of professional service he had been active in peace efforts on four continents.

One person in ten expressed joy that walls were coming down, that South Africa was ending apartheid. People of varied cultures were forming friendships, and members of various denominations were claiming their oneness in Christ. Maria, eighty-seven, said, "Within 100 feet of my door to the hall in this retirement home are members of four different denominations. I have learned to love them, pray with them, and give and receive mutual aid. Never before in my life was such unity true for me. I hope all Christ's followers may some day become one."

Mary Beth, eighty-three, said, "My son's wife divorced him, and now will not answer my calls or letters, but I will never give up my loving prayers to God for her good. I will win her love yet before I die. God is giving me these extra days. I feel God wants me to be a peacemaker in this borrowed time." Hope for peaceful resolution to conflict continues to energize her life and those of the other elderly.

A DEEP SPIRITUAL LIFE IS THE BASIS OF THE TRUEST HOPE

In a way too deep for words, many in this group of elderly hope to know God almost as intimately as Jesus did. They want to enter the kingdom with the naiveté of a child. They stake their soul for time and eternity on God's promises as being true. They believe that God hears and answers prayer and leads providentially, almost as if God sends a visible angel to do so. For many of them, spirituality is expressed by a new reality of God in liturgical responses, a new honesty in laughter, by prayer, by enjoying the stars, and by "smelling the roses" along the way.

The awareness of these elderly that they are drawing nearer to their death day enables this existential "I-Thou" immediacy with God. They speak about death almost as naturally as about parenting children. They see death as God's opening the door to a new and wonderful set of blessed realities. Death, to them, is merely "a turn in life's wheel." It is uniting with Jesus "in the home he has gone to prepare."

Repeatedly the interviewees mentioned how hymns or Scripture they had memorized long ago suddenly "connected" in a deeper way. They related humorous stories about loved ones now in heaven. Barry, eighty-two, said he had begun a second hour of Scripture reading and prayer every day. He asserted that for some reason he didn't grieve much when his aged friends died. "I already have more friends over there than I have here," he said. "I'm a little jealous that they have their glorified body and I must put up with this badly weakened one. The longing to be fully changed to be like Christ is increasing in me daily." He hoped for a peaceful homegoing.

Many of the persons interviewed had suffered many losses—of loved ones, jobs, homes, health, power, status, memory, identity, fitness, and meaning. They were quietly bracing themselves for still more loss and more pain and grief. But they nearly all implied that deeper spirituality leads to continued hope for this life. They wanted a greater empowering by God's Spirit, a deeper reality of eternal life, a simpler claiming of God's promises, a stronger trust in God's providence, and more praise arising to God at the climax of their prayers.

Not one of these eighty-year-olds claimed they should be exempt from their normal share of what happens to the aged. Only one expected a "secret rapture" to snatch him from human suffering. The majority longed for their sufferings to become as redemptive as Christ's.

Ike, eighty-three, who survived a serious cancer attack, said, "No matter how long I live, it will still be too short for all I'd love to do for my Lord."

Their lives say more profoundly than any creed can that

they have personalized Christ's death and resurrection, linking these truths to their own lives in a loving connection. In *Denial of Death* (Free Press, 1985), Ernest Becker speaks of the "cosmic heroism" of some aged. Many of these seventy-four have that cosmic heroism. They don't merely have a soul; they are a soul. They truly stand astride both this world and the next. They have courage to be. They live a centered life. Daily they take leaps of faith. They live by grace rather than by works. They have a deep sense of the holy. They know how to repent and to begin again by faith.

HUMOR AND A POSITIVE ATTITUDE NURTURE HOPE

A positive attitude may well be the main reason why the chaplains chose these persons as those whose life stories about hope would bless others. Some frankly stated, "I have decided to be a hopeful person." "I decided not to be a grouch," declared Homer, seventy-nine, with grim satisfaction. His was a life-or-death decision made before God.

The most hopeful aged were those who were determined to be hopeful persons at any cost. "I decided to join God's optimistic outlook," said Anita, seventy-seven. "I claimed Romans 8:28, where God decreed that all things will work together for good if I love my God and keep obeying his call. I decided to be positive about my near and long-range future." A Romans 8:28 motto hung prominently on her living room wall.

"I believe that, in the same degree in which my outer person is perishing, my inner core, my image of my God, is being renewed in Christlikeness," said Ralph, eighty-two, as he looked down at his feet. His body already showed sad limitations.

Interestingly, the seven who had never married showed a higher than average tendency to decide "to be a hopeful, positive person." All were deeply devoted to some cause of Christ's kingdom.

"I believe that I can direct my mind to sift out the good memories and to forget the abuses, hurts and failures," said Ruth, eighty-one. She quoted a verse from Philippians, "forgetting those things which are behind and pressing toward the mark for the prize Christ has for me. . . . I hope that from now on life is this much fun," she said.

"One reason I am hopeful now, even though the eyes and voice I used as a pastor-missionary are failing fast, is that I have learned throughout my long lifetime that whenever God closed one door, he opened a better one," said Richard, eighty-one, with confident joy in tone and body language. "I have decided, with every power of my will, that I'm going to see the good potential in people, rather than the bad." This sounded like a memorized speech or even a vow as he said it.

The most inspiringly hopeful aged were those who had made up their minds, apparently already in mid-life, that they would not accept that old age meant regressing downward from whatever stage in life at which they had failed the most.

"I'll soar like an eagle, just by learning how to tilt my wings into the winds," said Fred, eighty-six, in a wheelchair. "I will find the way to be gracious to my wife who insists that she will care for me. We've decided that whoever can push the wheelchair will be 'head' of the home." His wife, who overheard his humorous remark, joined him in hearty laughter.

TO THINK AND TALK ABOUT

1. What hopes did your parents have for you? What did your Creator have in mind for you?

2. Hope is a mystery to many. They can't decide if you learn it, earn it, or receive it by grace as you do salvation. What do you think?

3. If God gives you added years, beyond the usual three score and ten, what do you hope to do with them?

4. How should Christ's resurrection affect our hopes for life beyond death?

5. How can children and young persons be encouraged to be hopeful persons? Which of Miller's seven points begin in early life?

THE WRITERS

HELEN WADE ALDERFER, Goshen, Indiana, continues in retirement to write, speak, and teach. She especially enjoys teaching classes on "Writing Your Own Story." For twenty-five years she served as an editor at the Mennonite Publishing House, working on *Christian Living* and *On the Line*. She and husband Ed are the parents of five adult children and three grandchildren. They enjoy rug-hooking (Helen), beekeeping (Ed), and gardening and cooking together.

RICHARD GERBRANDT has been a pastor with the Mennonite Brethren for thirty-five years, serving with the Board of Christian Education, as church planter, senior pastor, and associate pastor. He is currently serving the Mennonite Brethren Church of Reedley, California, as minister of pastoral care.

WILLARD S. KRAYBILL, a retired physician living in Goshen, Indiana, is presently a consultant for Mennonite Mutual Aid. He served with Mennonite Central Committee in Vietnam, was college physician at Goshen College for twenty-four years, and now serves as executive secretary of the Mennonite Medical Association.

PAUL M. MILLER of Lititz, Pennsylvania, is enjoying voluntary service. He spends his time in pastoral counseling, assisting in the training of pastors in Supervised Pastoral Education programs, and in the Pastoral Care Department of Philhaven Hospital, all on a volunteer basis. Most of all, he enjoyed interviewing the seventy-four eighty-year-old "hopefuls."

LABAN and HELEN PEACHEY reside in Harrisonburg, Virginia, where he is campus pastor and director of placement at Eastern Mennonite Seminary, after working several years with Mennonite Mutual Aid as vice president of marketing. Helen has been active in various capacities with nursing homes in Hesston, Kansas, and Goshen, Indiana. She is secretary of the Virgina Women's Missionary and Service Commission.

DWIGHT E. ROTH has taught at Hesston College, Hesston, Kansas, in the social science department since 1973. His main academic interests include the influence of modernization upon the aging process, spiritual aspects of aging, and interreligious dialogue. He and his wife, Lynette Thiessen Roth, have one daughter.

MAYNARD SHELLY was an editor for the Commission on Education of the General Conference Mennonite Church for twenty-two years, which also included eleven years as editor of *The Mennonite*. He is the author of the *Discovery Bible Survey Course* (Faith and Life Press). In his retirement he is a free-lance writer and editor with special interest in Bible study and Mennonite history.

JAMES H. WALTNER is minister of College Mennonite Church, Goshen, Indiana. He has served pastorates in Kansas, California, and Illinois. He has been active in denominational work in both the General Conference and the Mennonite Church. He and his wife, Lenore Pankratz Waltner, have three grown children and one grandson.

KATIE FUNK WIEBE, professor emeritus of Tabor College, Hillsboro, Kansas, is a free-lance writer and editor living in Wichita, Kansas. She has a keen interest in her own aging and in being a cheerleader for older adults. She has written numerous books, including *Bless Me Too, My Father* and *Good Times with Old Times: How to Write Your Memoirs,* and hundreds of articles.

A Selected Bibliography

Becker, Arthur. *Ministry with Older Persons*. Augsburg, 1986.

*Bender, David and Bruno Leone, eds. *The Elderly: Opposing Viewpoints.*

Butler, Robert N. *Why Survive? Being Old in America.* Harper, 1985.

*Carlson, Avis D. *In the Fullness of Time: The Pleasures and Inconveniences of Growing Old.* Regnery, 1977.

Christian Living. March/April 1982 (a special focus on aging).

Clements, William M., ed. *Ministry with the Aging.* Harper, 1983.

*Cowley, Malcolm. *The View from 80.* Viking, 1980.

*Dulin, Rachel Z. *A Biblical View of Aging: A Crown of Glory.* Paulist, 1988.

Dychtwald, Ken and Joe Flower. *Age Wave: The Challenges and Opportunities of an Aging America.* Tarcher, 1989.

Erikson, Erik H., Joan M. Erickson and Helen Q. Kivnick. *Vital Involvement in Old Age: The Experience of Old Age in Our Time.* Norton, 1989.

Fletcher, William. *Recording Your Family History.* Dodd, Mead. 1989.

Geissler, Eugene. *The Best Is Yet to Be.* Ave Maria, 1988.

*Gerber, Jerry, Janet Wolff, Walter Klores and Gene Brown. *Lifetrends: The Future of Baby Boomers and Other Aging Americans.* MacMillan, 1989.

*Gray, Robert M. and David O. Moberg. *The Church and the Older Person.* Eerdmans, 1977.

Greshem, Perry E. *With Wings As Eagles*. Anna Publishing, 1980.

The Growing Silver Resource: Functional Approach for Congregational Involvement with the Elderly. Western District Conference of General Conference Mennonite Church, 1989.

Harder, Bertha, ed. *Young or Old or In Between: An Intergenerational Study on Aging*. Faith and Life, 1986.

Holmes, D. Lowell. *Other Cultures, Elder Years*. Burgess, 1983.

Hulme, William E. *Vintage Years: Growing Older with Meaning and Hope*. Westminster, 1986.

*Janss, Edmund. *Making the Second Half the Best Half*. Bethany, 1984.

*Kanin, Ruth. *Write the Story of Your Life*. Genealogical Publication, 1981.

Kerr, Horace L. *How to Minister to Senior Adults in Your Church*. Broadman, 1980.

Moody, Harry R. *Ethics in an Aging Society*. John Hopkins University Press, 1992.

Nouwen, Henri J.M. and Walter J. Gaffney. *Aging: The Fulfillment of Life*. Doubleday, 1976.

"Past Stories: Present Faith," *All God's People* video series. A collection of stories exploring past events that continue to shape present faith. Mennonite Media Ministries, Harrisonburg, Virginia.

Scott-Maxwell, Florida. *The Measure of My Days*. Viking, 1979.

Silverman, Philip, ed. *The Elderly as Modern Pioneers*. Indiana University Press, 1988

Simundson, Daniel J. *Hope for All Seasons: Biblical Expressions of Confidence in the Promises of God*. Augsburg, 1988.

Sinclair, Donna. *Worth Remembering.* Resource, 1988.

Smith, Tilman. *In Favor of Growing Older.* Herald, 1981.

Stagg, Frank. *The Bible Speaks on Aging.* Broadman, 1981.

Tournier, Paul. *Learning to Grow Old.* Harper, 1973.

Welch, Elizabeth. *Learning to Be 85.* Upper Room, 1991.

Whitehead, Evelyn Eaton and James D. Whitehead. *Christian Life Patterns: The Psychological Challenges and Religious Invitations of Adult Life.* Doubleday, 1982.

Wiebe, Katie Funk. *Bless Me Too, My Father.* Herald, 1988.

Wiebe, Katie Funk. *Good Times with Old Times: How to Write Your Memoirs.* Herald, 1979.

* Currently out of print, but may be available in your library.

FOR MORE INFORMATION ON AGING IN THE FAITH COMMUNITY:

Mennonite Association of Retired Persons is an organization dedicated to helping Mennonites share in the joy and potential of aging. It is a ministry of the Inter-Mennonite Council on Aging, P.O. Box 1245, Elkhart, Indiana 46515-1245.